Praise for *Duino*

"Alfred Corn's translation of Rilke's sublime work is the finest that I have ever read. It is, in a word, glorious. In it he captures the mystery, the depth, the terrifying beauty, and the compelling rhythm. He catches Rilke's voice, with its combined intimacy, power, and buoyancy, giving us words that rise from the page. In the preface, Corn takes us to the Duino Castle, where Rilke began writing the *Elegies*, presenting its rooms in vivid detail. This version assures us definitively that the *Duino Elegies*, despite their title, are celebratory, having far more to do with life and love than with death."

—Grace Schulman, author of *The Marble Bed*

"Rilke's *Duino Elegies*, composed a century ago in a fit of creative passion, gives voice to the modern predicament of inhabiting a world we endow with meaning yet find disturbingly recalcitrant to yield it back. Corn's subtle and sinuous translation lets Rilke sing in English with the sensual undertones and lyrical precision that lend this masterpiece of world literature such resonance even today."

—Ulrich Baer, translator and editor of *The Dark Interval: Rilke's Letters on Loss, Grief, and Transformation*

"Read Alfred Corn's new translation of Rilke's *Duino Elegies* and you will experience the lucid, precise, and musical results of an immensely demanding work undertaken by a gifted poet. Rilke was fascinated by the roots of words, by the metaphors that underlie German thought. Corn pays close attention to those metaphors, choosing Anglo-Saxon equivalents where possible, and his translation, like the original, is as much about language as it is about ideas."

—Scott Abbott, professor of integrated studies, philosophy and humanities, Utah Valley University

DUINO
ELEGIES

 Rainer Maria Rilke

DUINO
ELEGIES

A NEW AND COMPLETE TRANSLATION

TRANSLATED FROM THE GERMAN BY

Alfred Corn

W. W. NORTON & COMPANY
Independent Publishers Since 1923

To Grace Schulman, fellow Rilkean

For information about permission to reproduce selections from this book,
write to Permissions, W. W. Norton & Company, Inc.,
500 Fifth Avenue, New York, NY 10110

For information about special discounts for bulk purchases,
please contact W. W. Norton Special Sales at
specialsales@wwnorton.com or 800-233-4830

Manufacturing by LSC Communications Harrisonburg
Book design by Brooke Koven
Production manager: Julia Druskin

ISBN: 978-1-324-00540-7

W. W. Norton & Company, Inc., 500 Fifth Avenue, New York, N.Y. 10110
www.wwnorton.com

W. W. Norton & Company Ltd., 15 Carlisle Street, London W1D 3BS

1 2 3 4 5 6 7 8 9 0

CONTENTS

TRANSLATOR'S PREFACE

Late in January of 1912, Rainer Maria Rilke was a guest at Duino Castle outside Trieste, when the city was still a part of the Austro-Hungarian Empire. His hostess, the arts patron Princess Marie von Thurn und Taxis, had departed a few weeks earlier for another of her residences, entrusting him to the care of a staff familiar with his routine. Rilke's state of mind was poor; in fact, for two years he had suffered from depression and felt only an intermittent impulse to write. It was a dry spell that had begun in 1910, just after the publication of *The Notebooks of Malte Laurids Brigge*, a lapse that continued until that day in 1912. A troublesome business letter arrived for him at Duino (we believe that he received it on January 21); then, after an irritated reading, he put it aside. He walked down to the terraces below Duino's walls, where fresh air and spectacular vistas out to the Gulf of Trieste were likely to clear his mind. A stiff wind was blowing, one that locals call the *bora*, and the streaming air registered with him as an outcry, the scream that was to open the *Duino Elegies*. He said to himself, "What is that? What is coming?" He took out a notebook he had on hand and wrote down a sentence, and then a few more. He returned to his room, wrote an answer to the troublesome letter, and began working on what was to become the First Elegy. By evening he had a complete draft of it.

That opening line brought by the wind was this startling question: *Wer, wenn ich schriee, hörte mich denn aus der Engel Ordnungen?* In this translation I render the sentence as: "For who, if I cried out, would ever hear me among the angels and archangels?" Other translations give something like, "Who, if I cried out, would hear me among the angels' orders?" But I'm not sure that contemporary readers are aware that biblical angels were ranked in a hierarchy, with seraphim at the top, archangels next, and angels and cherubim below them—a ranking that allows us to be more specific. Christian liturgy in English has consecrated the phrase "with angels and archangels, and all the company of heaven," and Rilke often drew on Christian story and diction even though he was not at all an orthodox believer. Sure enough, in the Second Elegy an archangel arrives, and angelic influences of the higher orders run through the entire sequence.

Another new feature in my version of the poem's opening is to begin with "For" as a translation of the word "denn," which comes later in the line and is often omitted in earlier translations. This postpones by a split second the drama of the interrogative pronoun "who," but it also lets us know that the conflict treated in the poem began in Rilke's mind even before any words came to him. We're able to imagine a mental debate of someone whose anxieties might have prompted him to call for help, even as he realizes that summoning an angel or an archangel might not bring comfort. Instead of enlisting angelic aid, he launches the poem by explaining why he should *not* call out to the angels. They might not hear his outcry, and, even if one of them did, the poet conceives of these divine emissaries as so potent that direct contact would cause him to dissolve or faint away. Their special power he terms a *stärkeren Dasein*, which means, literally, a "stronger being-there," though it is usually translated "stronger existence." The Latinate word "existence" is rather abstract, though, so I have rendered the phrase as "more strongly grounded being." Rilke's angels are conceived as being so solid, so forceful, that mundane actuality fades on contact with them. It strikes me as entirely possible that Rilke knew the writings of Meister Eckhart von Hochheim, the fourteenth-century mystic, who said, "The authorities teach that next to the first emanation, which is the Son coming out of the Father, the angels are most like God. And it may well be true, for the soul at its highest is formed like God; but an angel gives a closer idea of Him. That is all an angel is: an idea of God. For this reason, the angel was sent to the soul, so that the soul might be re-formed by it, to be the divine idea by which it was first conceived." In biblical tradition, seeing the face of God resulted in death, so, if the angelic orders are deity in epitome, we can understand why Rilke feared close encounters with them.

The next sentence of the First Elegy invokes a special sense of the beautiful, one that is inseparable from terror:

> For the beautiful is nothing other
> than the onset of what is terrifying, something we just
> barely withstand,
> and we're struck with wonder at how calmly it disdains
> to destroy us.

All other versions translate *das Schöne* as "beauty," which is the correct translation of the word *die Schönheit*. But the adjectival neuter noun *das Schöne* means "the beautiful," a philosophical concept like "the true, "the virtuous," "the eternal." For Rilke, real things in the real world achieve fullness of being only when they are raised to an inward, metaphysical status, the realm of pure ideas. Note that he does the same with the adjectival noun *das Schreckliche* (here, in the genitive case, "des Schrecklichen") always translated before now as "terror," even though, more accurately, it means "the terrifying." Rilke's sense of the beautiful is imbued with the sublime, a category that Longinus and then Edmund Burke taught us to see as a blend of beauty and terror. What is beautiful begins, in a flash, by terrifying us. In one moment, the angel brings together the idea of the divine and the beautiful, a double revelation that the poet anticipates as a shattering encounter.

The opening of the poem is lit by an eerie radiance, the sort that awe brings on. Struck with beauty and terror, yet still intact, Rilke continues with the rest of the First Elegy; then a second, then a third, then a fourth. But the conclusion of the entire sequence was not set down until February 1922, an exalted month during which the poet also completed the *Sonnets to Orpheus*. A disastrous world war had intervened between the beginning of the work and its completion; despised military service had been inflicted on a rather frail poet; the pain of exile had deepened; and poor health had taken its toll. Even so, we don't need to cite those negatives as an explanation for the poet's decision concerning a title for the sequence. He began writing it at Duino Castle while enjoying the patronage of the owner, to whom the sequence is dedicated. As for the term "elegy," Rilke could call on the precedent of Goethe's *Römische Elegien* (*Roman Elegies*), which, like the elegies of Latin literature, were not laments for the dead but instead love poems. In any case, an elegy in classical poetry designated not the content of a poem, but only its meter—that is, alternating lines of iambic hexameter and pentameter. Several instances of this alternation occur in the work, but not often enough to qualify as its governing meter. In fact, there is no consistent metrical pattern throughout, though the Fourth and Eighth Elegies are composed in unrhymed iambic pentameter. The meter has been ignored in most previous translations, but I have restored it in this one. So far as I know, Rilke's decision to use blank verse for the Fourth and Eighth Elegies hasn't been the subject of any critical discussion; yet both poems deal with instances of restriction and confinement, and meter has, in the European tradition, often been figured as a signifier for hindrance or imprisonment of one sort or another, just as unmetered poetry is usually called "free verse."

If the Elegies are not lamentations for a deceased friend or beloved, no more are they love poems. Instead, they make a radical departure from a tradition that begins with the late medieval Italian poets of the *dolce stil nuovo*, influencers of Dante, who proposed that human love could be a path to redemption. Rilke, by contrast, sees human love as a hindrance, a "screen" interposed between the lovers and an authentic experience of the divine. Lovers tend to substitute each other for godhead, whereas these Elegies would have them look beyond human love to the most profound and encompassing vision available to us. Even so, Rilke venerates those lovers who love unrequitedly, the fullness and intensity of their devotion never being numbed by dailiness and mere practicality. Likewise, he has special regard for those who die young and thus don't experience severance from childhood and its seamless relationship to the external world. One way of understanding the Elegies is as a survey of various types of consciousness, human and animal, and the way these articulate with reality and with the divine. Privileged status is reserved for angels, who embody divine knowledge, but the poet sees children as possessing an exalted status as well, along with the early deceased and unrequited lovers. Rilke is also in sympathy with animals, praising their direct, unreflective engagement with nature, a focus on the present moment that frees them from the fear of death. It's a freedom that human consciousness cannot duplicate. Notice, too, that the Vegetable Kingdom prompts Rilke's admiration. Not only trees of noble stature, which figure in many of his poems, but even the lowly fig, which is celebrated in the Sixth Elegy's opening:

> Fig-tree, for a long time it's had meaning for me,
> the way you almost entirely get round your flowering
> and, with no pretension, urge your pristine secrecy
> into a fruit that early on takes a determined form.

This renders the German:

> Feigenbaum, seit wie lange schon ists mir bedeutend,
> wie du die Blüte beinah ganz überschlägst
> und hinein in die zeitig entschlossene Frucht,
> ungerühmt, drängst dein reines Geheimnis.

Rilke knows that stamens of the fig flower develop inside a fleshy envelope that eventually becomes the fruit. Pollination occurs when a species of wasp penetrates a tiny opening in that green vessel to reach its sugary interior. Once pollinated, the envelope swells and ripens into the fig we consume. The verb *überschlagen* (used here in the second-person present tense "überschlägst") means "wrap around," "enfold," and describes the way the fruit encloses its flower; but the verb also means "get past," "go beyond." The equivalent I found is "get round," and it is this dual action of the developing fig that intrigues Rilke, who admires a fruit that in part precedes its flower, enfolds it, and hides the developing seeds within as it continues past the flowering phase. This amounts to a botanical emblem for the kind of inwardness that the poet values, and the concept of fruition as a kind of forward progression returns in the Sixth Elegy when he speaks of women who conceive and give birth to heroes. The theme appears again in the Eighth Elegy, where the topic of animal pregnancy comes up.

I've said that the Elegies are not eulogies for a deceased person, but the Tenth Elegy could be understood as a premonitory mourning song intoned by Rilke for himself. He may have sensed in 1922 that he was not far from his own death, which came four years later. The poet begins with the hope that his singing might one day win approval from the angels and concludes with the description of an eerie encounter between a young man who has recently died and a woman member of a tribe he calls the Lamentations. This figure describes the conditions the young man should expect in his new habitation. A voice both personal and authorial returns to end the poem with some uncanny speculations:

> Yet if the eternally dead should alert us to a resemblance,
> then consider that they might be gesturing towards the
> catkins,
> those hanging

down from leafless hazels, or else
might mention rain that falls on dark soil early in the
                                                         year.—

And we who always thought of good fortunes
as *rising*, would experience an emotion
that almost astounds us
when we see a fortunate thing that *falls*.

We are accustomed to associating any welcome celebration with an upward trajectory, an ascent toward Heaven. But Rilke's suggestion here is that the well-lived, praiseworthy life, when it comes to its end, *falls*; it drops down to earth like the seeds of a plant, along with life-giving rain. The implication is that the good death is involved in a reseeding of the earth—just as the fruit of the fig precedes its seeds and then releases them at the moment of maturity and consummation.

To point out the impossibility of providing a full and adequate preface for a work like the *Duino Elegies* isn't a bid for sympathy but simply an echo of what the author himself acknowledged. In a letter to Marie von Thurn und Taxis, Rilke spoke of "the infinite, unavoidable difficulties which these verses present, not so much because of their obscurity but because the point of departure is often concealed, like roots in the ground." Farther on in the letter, as he notes a kinship between the Elegies and the *Sonnets to Orpheus*, he says, "It's not really possible to suggest just how far one is able to carry oneself over into the dense, artful fabric of these elegies and individual sonnets; often it's strange for the author's disposition to feel, on his more diminished days (and so many of them are that), so close to the essence of his own life in its overwhelming ineffability" (*Briefe*, vol. II, p. 448, Aug. 9, 1924).

Much that we find moving in the Elegies is developed in the realm of the inexpressible, no matter that the inexpressible is fused with and inseparable from the language in which the poems are composed. I would say that at least half the content we discern, as we try to penetrate the poems' aura of mystery, consists of the words themselves, their sonority and rhythm, coordinated in the elaborate syntax characteristic of German language. To state the obvious: no translation of great poetry equals the original. A major poem's intrinsic, idiomatic virtues make that impossible; in fact, the greater the poem, the less likely it is that a translation can do it full justice. Yet this blunt truth has never prevented commenters from remarking that a translation has failed to convey all that is found in the original. It can't; but that is not to say that we should simply throw up our hands and leave world masterpieces in their original language. Readers who don't know ancient Greek want to glimpse as through a partly opened door the achievement of Sappho and Sophocles; those who don't read Russian want to approach Pushkin and Akhmatova; and those without German want to get some idea of the greatness of Kafka and Rilke. That sector of the readership passionately devoted to a foreign-language author won't fail to read several translations cooperatively. A translation is always an interpretation, and great poems allow different readings. I urge Rilke's sincerest admirers, if they want a full sense of the possibilities, to read this new translation along with some of the other extant versions, several of which are good. I'm aware that, just as we usually like the first version of a song more than the later "covers," we seldom allow a new translation to override our affection for the first version we came to know. Even if it doesn't in every case displace for us the old, a new translation can nevertheless bring fresh perspectives to bear; and a work as great as the *Duino Elegies* deserves a renewed and careful engagement instead of a merely reflexive admiration.

I first encountered Rilke's poetry as an undergraduate during my second-year German studies. This was the lyric Rilke, author of memorable short poems like "Archaic Torso of Apollo," "The Panther," and "Autumn Day." In some sense Rilke's ringing command at the conclusion of the "Archaic Torso of Apollo" did in fact have its intended effect. The last word is *ändern*, "change," and I believe I sought, after reading it, to begin a life different from the one I had been living. The decision brought with it, first, the very *willingness* to change, and not to become mired in comfortable, unexamined routine. That decision led to changes of many different kinds and may even explain my readiness to give new versions of translations that have become ingrained in the readership's consciousness. In most versions of the "Archaic Torso," for example, the last sentence is rendered as "You must change your life." Accurate, but not metrical; further, it makes the last word of the sonnet "life," rather than Rilke's "change." The way I rendered it, in iambic meter, is, "The life you led before must change." And yet, something is still lost. The sound of the word *ändern* in German is almost indistinguishable from the verb *enden*, which means "end." That verb ends the poem. There is the uncanny suggestion that the change is a kind of death, one that we must choose. Rilke's greatest poems are never far from the uncanny.

As an undergraduate I heard the *Duino Elegies* mentioned, but I did not attempt to read them until nearly a decade after my first encounter with Rilke. Even with the

Leishman-Spender translation on hand, there was the sense that I had not grasped all that the Elegies contained. It was a goal that would require not only a further study of Rilke, but also the condition of being an older reader, one with more life experience. In subsequent years I read his lyrics, but also Rilke's prose, including his *Letters to a Young Poet* and the astonishing *Notebooks of Malte Laurids Brigge*. When I began publishing my own poetry, it felt as though his example had been influential, just as it had been for contemporary American poets like James Wright, Robert Bly, Galway Kinnell, James Merrill, and Grace Schulman. Some of my own books included translations of his lyrics, and I have added them to the present volume, along with two of the *Letters to a Young Poet*.

Those letters have become a celebrated part of Rilke's ocuvre even though he didn't collect and publish them himself. That was done three years after Rilke's death by the recipient, an Austrian named Franz Xaver Kappus, who was only nineteen years of age in 1902, when he first wrote to Rilke. The established poet might reasonably have ignored Kappus's letter, given that they weren't acquainted; but Kappus was a cadet at the Theresian Military Academy near Vienna, an institution in whose lower division Rilke himself had been forced to enroll many years earlier. This incidental connection and Kappus's sincerely expressed desire to write poetry may explain why the correspondence began and continued for six years. Rilke declined to offer criticisms of Kappus's efforts or to offer technical instruction. Instead, his approach resembles psychological counseling— an eloquent portrayal of the attitudes and goals the beginner must acquire in order to write with authenticity and originality. The focus is always on inwardness and on the courage needed to confront what introspection discovers. The sixth and eighth letters, written in 1903 and 1904, also contain ideas and themes that eventually came to full, poetic expression in the *Duino Elegies*. As such, they are an indication of the continuity that runs throughout all Rilke's work.

In January of 2012, I was a Visiting Fellow at Clare Hall, Cambridge; the project I had chosen for my stay was to translate the Elegies. Late in my career as a poet, late in life, I surmised that it was time to become intimately acquainted with one of the greatest modern treatments of the theme of death. I said to myself, "It's now or never." I arrived in Cambridge almost exactly a century after Rilke drafted the First Elegy and set to work. Then, in April, I made a pilgrimage to Trieste, with the plan of visiting Duino Castle during the stay. Wandering about a city whose history extends from the Roman to the Austro-Hungarian Empire and beyond, I noticed a fountain in the Piazza della Borsa, with a sculptural group that featured Neptune holding a metal trident— no doubt a reminder of the Adriatic Sea beside which Trieste was founded, and the source of its prosperity. I wondered if this sculpture was one of the prompts for the Third Elegy, as it invokes both Neptune and his signature implement. After all, when writers are engaged in a new project, the process of composition exercises magnetic attraction on details from the environment surrounding them.

I was also tempted to see a similar prompt in the Victory Lighthouse, a column supporting an angel that you see on the journey from Trieste to Duino. Yet that statue wouldn't have been seen by Rilke because it wasn't put in place until 1927. One can't help wondering if, in this case, the prompt goes the other way. The *Duino Elegies* were published in 1923, just as ground was broken for the Victory Lighthouse.

I don't know what deliberations were involved in its design, or whether Marie von Thurn und Taxis might have been consulted about it. It would be no surprise if we learned that she proposed the incorporation of an angel in the design, considering that the author of the poetic sequence dedicated to her (an author she sometimes affectionately called "Dottor Serafico") had died in 1926. The Victory Lighthouse angel is female and not terrifying, but that sort of error could be attributed to the public incomprehension that any serious poet soon learns to expect.

I arrived at Duino Castle on a sunny spring morning, and before entering the Castle gate first walked down to the terraces and gardens below its walls. Cypress trees, boxwood, lilacs, and a little fountain with sculpted cherubim at its center, angels not of an order high enough to be mentioned in Rilke's sequence. A ravishing prospect onto the sea took up most of my attention. Perhaps not strong enough to be termed a *bora*, there was even so a wind coming in from the Adriatic, and I had no trouble recalling the opening sentence of the First Elegy as breezes lightly buffeted my ears. I came to a fenced-off stone table where a plaque informed the public that Rilke had written his Elegies there—a bit of tourist-attraction license, as he never said that the work had been composed outdoors. No matter. I went into the Castle, inspected the rooms, including Princess Marie's bedroom, the library, the dining hall. Unoccupied by its owners, just as when Rilke began his poem, the interior seemed immutable, as though the intervening century had been whisked away without noticeable changes to anything on view. I know nothing about ghosts, but a good substitute for haunting was the certainty that nearly all the objects before my eyes had been seen by Rilke during his several stays. In my mind that fact left a layer of implication on the Castle's books and furniture, one not quite describable, yet part of their *Dasein*.

The coda for my exploration of significant Rilke sites came three years later when at the invitation of Professor Thomas Austenfeld I came to the University of Fribourg for a presentation of my work as a poet. Once that was done, he kindly volunteered to drive me, in the company of a graduate student named Ola Madhour, to the village of Raron in the Swiss canton of Valais. There, high up above the town, we found the Burgkirche of St. Michael's, where Rilke is buried. The tomb is found outside the church, against its southern wall. We paused to read his famously enigmatic epitaph:

Rose, oh reiner Widerspruch, Lust,
niemandes Schlaf zu sein unter soviel
Lidern.

Rose, oh pure self-contradiction, pleasure,
to be no one's sleep under so many
eyelids.

The rose, literal and figurative, is a recurrent motif in Rilke's poetry, and an early letter mentions that he had discovered a new caress: placing a rose lightly on someone's closed eyelid. Here the paradox (or self-contradiction) is that the petals of the rose are like eyelids, yet there are no eyes underneath, and therefore no sleeping eyes. The final phase of Rilke's illness (he suffered from leukemia for some time before it was diagnosed) began when the scratch he received from a rose thorn developed into an infection his impaired immune system couldn't combat. The epitaph concludes with a punning word *Lidern* ("eyelids"), its sound almost indistinguishable from *Lieder*, which means "songs." In fact, the singular forms of both nouns, *Lid* and *Lied*, sound exactly the same. We might also hear a homophonic pun in the adjective *reiner*, sonically identical to the poet's first name. The rose has traditionally served as a figure for the feminine, so it is strange to see it on the tomb of a man. Yet an even more ancient personification is the Earth as our mother. She gives birth to us, and when we die we return to her womb. A possible suggestion in the epitaph is that, bald facts aside, there will have been no sleep of death under the lid of the gravestone. The poet's "songs" live and are still being sung, just as Rilke has "become his admirers," as Auden once put it. The tomb is a tomb but a self-contradictory one, attesting to life as much as death. To offer this interpretation does not, of course, exhaust all the possibilities.

From the church of St. Michael we drove several miles to the Château de Muzot, a residence lent to Rilke by a patron during the last years of his life. Built of stone on two levels, and not notably spacious, the house doesn't conform to anyone's stock image of a castle. Nevertheless, Rilke said he was happy to have this shelter, a happiness experienced partly because the house was isolated enough to allow for uninterrupted work. In an astonishing burst of creative energy, he completed the last of the Elegies there in the same month when the *Sonnets to Orpheus* were written. In a February 1922 letter to Lou Andreas-Salomé, he described this period of furious creation as "an untrammeled storm, a hurricane of the spirit, and everything inside me, like cords and webbing or frames, all of it, is split and twisted" (Rainer Maria Rilke and Lou Andreas-Salomé, *Briefwechsel*, p. 464). It would be a mistake to assume that the rapidity of composition accounts for the difficulty of these poems. In a letter to Nanny von

Escher, he says, "Yet it is in the nature of these poems, their condensation and brevity of expression (the way they often speak in lyric totals rather than itemizing the tropes necessary for the sum), that they seem conceived overall to be understood more by those who are pulled in this same direction than only by what we regard as 'understanding.' Two of my most compelling inner convictions were central to their making: the intention, which more and more gained strength in my mind, to open life up to death; and, besides that, the spiritual imperative to place representations of love in a broader context than had ever been possible in the stricter confines of life as such (which excludes death as being totally Other)" (*Rainer Maria Rilke: Briefe*, vol. II, p. 330).

Orpheus returns from the Underworld to sing his lament, but in short order he is torn limb from limb, his severed head still singing as it flows on the river currents where it was flung. Rilke, still residing in the Château Muzot, died in 1926, leaving a body of work of great depth and variety, including the ten Elegies that have more to do with celebration than bereavement, more to do with life than with death. The last word of the sequence is "falls," but it is the kind of self-contradictory fall that, like the sun, also rises. It does that every morning of the world.

Rhode Island, February 2019

DUINESER ELEGIEN

THE DUINO ELEGIES

Aus dem Besitz der Fürstin
Marie von Thurn und Taxis-Hohenlohe

Among the possessions of Princess
Marie von Thurn und Taxis-Hohenlohe

Die erste Elegie

Wer, wenn ich schriee, hörte mich denn aus der Engel
Ordnungen? und gesetzt selbst, es nähme
einer mich plötzlich ans Herz: ich verginge von seinem
stärkeren Dasein. Denn das Schöne ist nichts
als des Schrecklichen Anfang, den wir noch grade ertragen,
und wir bewundern es so, weil es gelassen verschmäht,
uns zu zerstören. Ein jeder Engel ist schrecklich.
    Und so verhalt ich mich denn und verschlucke den Lockruf
dunkelen Schluchzens. Ach, wen vermögen
wir denn zu brauchen? Engel nicht, Menschen nicht,
und die findigen Tiere merken es schon,
daß wir nicht sehr verläßlich zu Haus sind
in der gedeuteten Welt. Es bleibt uns vielleicht
irgend ein Baum an dem Abhang, daß wir ihn täglich
wiedersähen; es bleibt uns die Straße von gestern
und das verzogene Treusein einer Gewohnheit,
der es bei uns gefiel, und so blieb sie und ging nicht.
    O und die Nacht, die Nacht, wenn der Wind voller
                                  Weltraum
uns am Angesicht zehrt -, wem bliebe sie nicht, die
ersehnte, sanft enttäuschende, welche dem einzelnen Herzen
mühsam bevorsteht. Ist sie den Liebenden leichter?
Ach, sie verdecken sich nur mit einander ihr Los.
    Weißt du's *noch* nicht? Wirf aus den Armen die Leere
zu den Räumen hinzu, die wir atmen; vielleicht daß die Vögel
die erweiterte Luft fühlen mit innigerm Flug.

Ja, die Frühlinge brauchten dich wohl. Es muteten manche
Sterne dir zu, daß du sie spürtest. Es hob

4

The First Elegy

For who, if I cried out, would ever hear me among the angels
and archangels? And even if one of them did suddenly
crush me against his heart, I would dissolve, undone by his more
strongly grounded being. For the beautiful is nothing other
than the onset of what is terrifying, something we just
                                        barely withstand,
and we're struck with wonder at how calmly it disdains
to destroy us. Every one of the angels is terrifying.
    So I stand up straight, swallow, and choke back the birdcall
that my twilight sobbing became. Ah, but who could be
expected to fill our needs? Not angels, not people,
and the more attentive animals have already noticed
that we are not dependably at home
in an interpreted world. Perhaps there remains for us
a tree somewhere on a hillside, one we daily see;
streets from bygone eras remain,
and the boorish loyalty of a habit that so
liked living with us, it remained and never left.
    Oh, and Night, Night, when a wind filled with the cosmos
tears at one's face—, for whom would it not remain, longed-for,
mildly disappointing, an arduous prospect
for the heart in solitude. Does it rest more lightly on lovers?
Ah, they only mask themselves in each other to conceal their fate.
    Do you *still* not understand? Let your arms fling absences
outward to the space we breathe in; it may well be that birds
will meet the ampler air with a flight even more passionate.

Yes, those early springs did need you. How many stars
have urged you to become aware of them. A wave

5

sich eine Woge heran im Vergangenen, oder
da du vorüberkamst am geöffneten Fenster,
gab eine Geige sich hin. Das alles war Auftrag.
Aber bewältigtest du's? Warst du nicht immer
noch von Erwartung zerstreut, als kündigte alles
eine Geliebte dir an? (Wo willst du sie bergen,
da doch die großen fremden Gedanken bei dir
aus und ein gehn und öfters bleiben bei Nacht.)
Sehnt es dich aber, so singe die Liebenden; lange
noch nicht unsterblich genug ist ihr berühmtes Gefühl.
Jene, du neidest sie fast, Verlassenen, die du
so viel liebender fandst als die Gestillten. Beginn
immer von neuem die nie zu erreichende Preisung;
denk: es erhält sich der Held, selbst der Untergang war ihm
nur ein Vorwand, zu sein: seine letzte Geburt.
Aber die Liebenden nimmt die erschöpfte Natur
in sich zurück, als wären nicht zweimal die Kräfte,
dieses zu leisten. Hast du der Gaspara Stampa
denn genügend gedacht, daß irgend ein Mädchen,
dem der Geliebte entging, am gesteigerten Beispiel
dieser Liebenden fühlt: daß ich würde wie sie?
Sollen nicht endlich uns diese ältesten Schmerzen
fruchtbarer werden? Ist es nicht Zeit, daß wir liebend
uns vom Geliebten befrein und es bebend bestehn:
wie der Pfeil die Sehne besteht, um gesammelt im Absprung
mehr zu sein als er selbst. Denn Bleiben ist nirgends.

Stimmen, Stimmen. Höre, mein Herz, wie sonst nur
Heilige hörten: daß die der riesige Ruf
aufhob vom Boden; sie aber knieten,
Unmögliche, weiter und achtetens nicht:

from long ago rose up towards you, or,
as you approached an opened window,
a violin handed itself over. All this was your mission.
But were you equal to it? Weren't you constantly
distracted by anticipation, as though everything
foretold a new beloved? (What refuge can you
offer her, while all those vast, alien thoughts stray
in and out, at times staying overnight.) Still,
if yearning should come, then sing of lovers; their renowned
passion is not even close to being immortal enough.
The forsaken—you almost envy them—struck you
as much more loving than the requited. Reach again and again
toward the never fully attained goal of proclaiming their worth.
Reflect: the hero always persists, even his downfall
proved to be only a brief illusion: a definitive birth.
But lovers are reabsorbed by depleted Nature as though
her energies could never manage to form them
a second time. Have you done all you could to venerate
Gaspara Stampa, so that any young woman abandoned
by her lover, when pondering the high example
of this passionate person, will feel: Let me become what she was?
Shouldn't these, our oldest torments, at last become
more fruitful? Isn't it time for us, though still loving,
to free ourselves from the beloved, and, trembling, stand firm:
as an arrow stands firm on the string, and, mustered into the
                                                    rebound,
becomes more than itself. For standing still is being nowhere.

Voices, voices. Listen, heart, as before now only
the saints have listened: thus the immense summons
lifted them from the ground; but continuing
to kneel, these more than human beings never noticed:

7

So waren sie hörend. Nicht, daß du *Gottes* ertrügest
die Stimme, bei weitem. Aber das Wehende höre,
die ununterbrochene Nachricht, die aus Stille sich bildet.
Es rauscht jetzt von jenen jungen Toten zu dir.
Wo immer du eintratst, redete nicht in Kirchen
zu Rom und Neapel ruhig ihr Schicksal dich an?
Oder es trug eine Inschrift sich erhaben dir auf,
wie neulich die Tafel in Santa Maria Formosa.
Was sie mir wollen? leise soll ich des Unrechts
Anschein abtun, der ihrer Geister
reine Bewegung manchmal ein wenig behindert.

Freilich ist es seltsam, die Erde nicht mehr zu bewohnen,
kaum erlernte Gebräuche nicht mehr zu üben,
Rosen, und andern eigens versprechenden Dingen
nicht die Bedeutung menschlicher Zukunft zu geben;
das, was man war in unendlich ängstlichen Händen,
nicht mehr zu sein, und selbst den eigenen Namen
wegzulassen wie ein zerbrochenes Spielzeug.
Seltsam, die Wünsche nicht weiterzuwünschen. Seltsam,
alles, was sich bezog, so lose im Raume
flattern zu sehen. Und das Totsein ist mühsam
und voller Nachholn, daß man allmählich ein wenig
Ewigkeit spürt. - Aber Lebendige machen
alle den Fehler, daß sie zu stark unterscheiden.
Engel (sagt man) wüßten oft nicht, ob sie unter
Lebenden gehn oder Toten. Die ewige Strömung
reißt durch beide Bereiche alle Alter
immer mit sich und übertönt sie in beiden.

Schließlich brauchen sie uns nicht mehr, die Früheentrückten,
man entwöhnt sich des Irdischen sanft, wie man den Brüsten

that *was* their listening. Not that you could withstand
the voice of God—far from. But hear the blowing wind,
as its uninterrupted message develops out of silence.
It whispers to you now from those who died young.
Whenever you visited a church, in Rome or Naples,
didn't their destiny calmly speak to you?
Or an inscription extend to you its elevated relief
as one recently did on that tomb in Santa Maria Formosa?
What is it those dead ask of me? That I gently dispel
any implication of their being wronged, which sometimes
hinders, a little, their spirits' serene motion.

Granted, it's strange no longer to live on Earth,
no more to practice customs only recently acquired,
not lending to roses and other things strikingly
auspicious a meaning for our human future;
no more to be held in relentlessly anxious hands,
as you once were, and even your own name—
to let it drop like a broken toy.
Strange not to wish any further wishes. Strange
to see all that was once interlocked fly apart
and scatter through space. And being dead is hard work,
addressing a few remaining tasks, so that we may at last
taste eternity. But the living all make the same
mistake: they draw too sharp a distinction.
Angels (we're told) often didn't know whether they were
walking among the living or the dead. The eternal current
flowing through the two domains forever sweeps along
with it all ages, which its onrush drowns out in both.

Finally, they no longer need us, those spirited away early;
they quietly wean themselves from the habit of earthly things,

milde der Mutter entwächst. Aber wir, die so große
Geheimnisse brauchen, denen aus Trauer so oft
seliger Fortschritt entspringt -: *könnten* wir sein ohne sie?
Ist die Sage umsonst, daß einst in der Klage um Linos
wagende erste Musik dürre Erstarrung durchdrang;
daß erst im erschrockenen Raum, dem ein beinah göttlicher
Jüngling
plötzlich für immer enttrat, das Leere in jene
Schwingung geriet, die uns jetzt hinreißt und tröstet und hilft.

much as one outgrows the mother's tender breast. But we
who need great mysteries, we, whose grieving is so often
the source of imaginative gains—: could we truly live without
them?
Is that legend no help, telling how once during the lament for
Linos
a daring primal music cut through thickened apathy;
and a youth near to being a god suddenly and forever
stepped away from bewildered space, an absence turning
into that humming that sweeps us on, comforts, and supports.

Notes

Gaspara Stampa: Venetian poet (1523–1554), the author of *Rime*, some of whose poems record her unrequited love for Count Collaltino di Collalto. In Rilke's imagination she takes her place beside other exemplary fictional or historical women whose love went unrequited, such as the French Renaissance poet Louise Labé, Mariana Alcoforado (purported author of *Letters of a Portuguese Nun*, first published in French in 1669), and Bettina von Arnim, who engaged in a correspondence with Goethe.

Santa Maria Formosa: A Venetian church founded in the seventh century after a vision of the Virgin came to Saint Magnus, who saw her as a "shapely" (*formosa*) lady. The present church was built in 1492, its architect Mauro Codussi. Rilke and Princess Marie visited the church in April of 1911. The reference is made most likely to commemorative tablets on a large, elaborate tomb for the brothers Wilhelm and Anton Hellemans, Antwerp businessmen who died in Venice in the late sixteenth century. An inscription above the door speaks of charity for the poor and "immatura morte," that is, "premature death." Wilhelm's inscription is as follows: *Vixi aliis dum vita fuit / post funera tandem / Non perii, at gelido / in marmore vivo mihi. Guglielmus eram / Me Flandria luget / Hadria suspirat / pauperiesque vocat.* "While life was, I lived for others / then at last after death / I did not perish but frozen / in marble I live to myself. I was Wilhelm / Flanders mourns / the Adriatic Sea sighs / and poverty calls me."

Linos: The mythological son of Apollo and the epic Muse Calliope or else Terpsichore, Muse of the dance. He can be considered the mythological inventor of music and rhythm or simply the embodiment of a song of lamentation (the Greek word *linos* means "a dirge"). His myth is fragmentary, but in one version he was killed by Herakles, who struck him with a lyre because Linos had reproached him for mistakes in his performance. Rilke takes the myth a step farther and imagines that music was created out of the vibration that filled the absence left behind after Linos's departure.

Die zweite Elegie

Jeder Engel ist schrecklich. Und dennoch, weh mir,
ansing ich euch, fast tödliche Vögel der Seele,
wissend um euch. Wohin sind die Tage Tobiae,
da der Strahlendsten einer stand an der einfachen Haustür,
zur Reise ein wenig verkleidet und schon nicht mehr furchtbar;
(Jüngling dem Jüngling, wie er neugierig hinaussah).
Träte der Erzengel jetzt, der gefährliche, hinter den Sternen
eines Schrittes nur nieder und herwärts: hochauf-
schlagend erschlüg uns das eigene Herz. Wer seid ihr?

Frühe Geglückte, ihr Verwöhnten der Schöpfung,
Höhenzüge, morgenrötliche Grate
aller Erschaffung, - Pollen der blühenden Gottheit,
Gelenke des Lichtes, Gänge, Treppen, Throne,
Räume aus Wesen, Schilde aus Wonne, Tumulte
stürmisch entzückten Gefühls und plötzlich, einzeln,
Spiegel: die die entströmte eigene Schönheit
wiederschöpfen zurück in das eigene Antlitz.

Denn wir, wo wir fühlen, verflüchtigen; ach wir
atmen uns aus und dahin; von Holzglut zu Holzglut
geben wir schwächern Geruch. Da sagt uns wohl einer:
ja, du gehst mir ins Blut, dieses Zimmer, der Frühling
füllt sich mit dir . . . Was hilfts, er kann uns nicht halten,
wir schwinden in ihm und um ihn. Und jene, die schön sind,
o wer hält sie zurück? Unaufhörlich steht Anschein

The Second Elegy

Every angel terrifies. Though I shouldn't, I am singing
at *you*, all-but-lethal birds of the soul, in full knowledge
of what you can do. Where has it gone, the age of Tobias, when
                                  from
the realm of radiant beings just *one* stood at a plain front door,
partly disguised for the journey, and no longer frightening
(one young man curious about another young man, as he
                                  looked outside).
Now, if the archangel stepped like a threat from behind the stars
and took a single stride down towards us, our own pounding
heartbeat would slaughter us. Who could you be?

Joyous from the start, creation's favored companions,
upthrust heights, Earth's sierras tinged rose-red
at dawn,—pollen of flowering godhead,
cusps of light, hallways, stairs, thrones,
spaces made of Being, crests of rapture, cyclonic,
ravishing tumults, and suddenly, one at a time,
mirrors, each recreating itself in each while pouring
forth beauty into its own countenance.

For we, wherever we feel, diffuse, oh, we breathe
ourselves out and away; ember to glowing ember
we release a fading scent of smoke. Though someone might say:
Yes, you're seeping into my bloodstream, this room, this spring
is filling up with you . . . Does it matter? he can't hold on to us,
we vanish inside and all around him. And the loveliest:
who then is holding them back? Semblance constantly

auf in ihrem Gesicht und geht fort. Wie Tau von dem Frühgras
hebt sich das Unsre von uns, wie die Hitze von einem
heißen Gericht. O Lächeln, wohin? O Aufschaun:
neue, warme, entgehende Welle des Herzens -;
weh mir: wir *sinds* doch. Schmeckt denn der Weltraum,
in den wir uns lösen, nach uns? Fangen die Engel
wirklich nur Ihriges auf, ihnen Entströmtes,
oder ist manchmal, wie aus Versehen, ein wenig
unseres Wesens dabei? Sind wir in ihre
Züge so viel nur gemischt wie das Vage in die Gesichter
schwangerer Frauen? Sie merken es nicht in dem Wirbel
ihrer Rückkehr zu sich. (Wie sollten sie's merken.)

Liebende könnten, verstünden sie's, in der Nachtluft
wunderlich reden. Denn es scheint, daß uns alles
verheimlicht. Siehe, die Bäume *sind*; die Häuser,
die wir bewohnen, bestehn noch. Wir nur
ziehen allem vorbei wie ein luftiger Austausch.
Und alles ist einig, uns zu verschweigen, halb als
Schande vielleicht und halb als unsägliche Hoffnung.

Liebende, euch, ihr in einander Genügten,
frag ich nach uns. Ihr greift euch. Habt ihr Beweise?
Seht, mir geschiehts, daß meine Hände einander
inne werden oder daß mein gebrauchtes
Gesicht in ihnen sich schont. Das giebt mir ein wenig
Empfindung. Doch wer wagte darum schon zu *sein*?
Ihr aber, die ihr im Entzücken des anderen
zunehmt, bis er euch überwältigt
anfleht: nicht *mehr* -; die ihr unter den Händen
euch reichlicher werdet wie Traubenjahre;

rises up in their face and then departs. Dew from the grass
                                        at dawn,
what is ours lifts away from us, like warmth above
a steaming dish. O smile, where to? O upturned glance:
new, warm, receding ripple of the heart—;
alas, but that is what we are. Does the space we dissolve
into then taste of us? And is it true that angels
merely recapture their own, what they first poured out,
or sometimes, as though by mistake, a little
of our essence also? Are we an ingredient in their
features, much like that vagueness seen in the faces
of pregnant women? They don't notice it as they revolve
back into themselves. (How should they notice it?)

Lovers might, if they only understood, voice awe-inspiring
words to the night air. For it seems that everything wants
to hide us away. Look around you, the trees *exist*, the houses
we inhabit are still standing firm. It's only we
who let it all go by like some weightless exchange of breath.
And everything agrees not to speak of us, half out
of shame, maybe, and half out of ineffable hope.

You lovers, contented with one another, I'm asking you
about us. You cling to each other. What guarantees do you have?
You see, sometimes I find that my hands become
aware of themselves, or that my exhausted forehead
takes shelter in them. It gives me a fleeting
sensation. Yet who, just because of that, would claim to *be*?
You, though, who expand in each other's
rapture until, overpowered, one of you begs:
no *more*—; you who thrive under each other's hands
as sumptuously as grape clusters in a vintage year;

die ihr manchmal vergeht, nur weil der andre
ganz überhand nimmt: euch frag ich nach uns. Ich weiß,
ihr berührt euch so selig, weil die Liebkosung verhält,
weil die Stelle nicht schwindet, die ihr, Zärtliche,
zudeckt; weil ihr darunter das reine
Dauern verspürt. So versprecht ihr euch Ewigkeit fast
von der Umarmung. Und doch, wenn ihr der ersten
Blicke Schrecken besteht und die Sehnsucht am Fenster,
und den ersten gemeinsamen Gang, *ein* Mal durch den Garten:
Liebende, *seid* ihrs dann noch? Wenn ihr einer dem andern
euch an den Mund hebt und ansetzt -: Getränk an Getränk:
o wie entgeht dann der Trinkende seltsam der Handlung.

Erstaunte euch nicht auf attischen Stelen die Vorsicht
menschlicher Geste? war nicht Liebe und Abschied
so leicht auf die Schultern gelegt, als wär es aus anderm
Stoffe gemacht als bei uns? Gedenkt euch der Hände,
wie sie drucklos beruhen, obwohl in den Torsen die Kraft steht.
Diese Beherrschten wußten damit: so weit sind wirs,
dieses ist unser, uns *so* zu berühren; stärker
stemmen die Götter uns an. Doch dies ist Sache der Götter.

Fänden auch wir ein reines, verhaltenes, schmales
Menschliches, einen unseren Streifen Fruchtlands
zwischen Strom und Gestein. Denn das eigene Herz bersteigt
uns
noch immer wie jene. Und wir können ihm nicht mehr
nachschaun in Bilder, die es besänftigen, noch in
göttliche Körper, in denen es größer sich mäßigt.

who at times dwindle away only because the other
so strongly takes the lead. I'm asking you about us. I know,
you touch each other so ardently because the caress
holds fast: no place your hand rests on, tender souls,
ever vanishes; because under it you sense a pure
continuing. You exchange the promise of eternity almost
in your embrace alone. And yet, if you withstand
those first terrifying glances, your long vigil at the window,
and the first walk together, that *one* time through the garden:
Lovers, are you still all that you were? If both of you lift
each other to your lips and unite—: potion to potion:
oh how strangely those who are drinking elude that deed.

Didn't it astound you, the foresight of those human gestures
carved on Athenian grave markers, weren't love and farewell
laid on shoulders so lightly as to seem composed of a material
different from ours? Consider those hands, the way they rest
without pressure, no matter how strong the chest and shoulders.
Having mastered themselves, they acknowledged: we can go
                                        only so far,
this much is allowed, to touch one another just this way.
                                    The gods can
press down on us with more strength. But that is the gods'
                                        prerogative.

We would like to find something pure, contained, spare,
human, our one and only strip of fruitful land between
river and rock. For our own heart climbs beyond us
just as theirs always did. And no longer can our eyes
follow it into images, which soothe it, nor even into
godlike bodies, where it gains greater self-control.

Notes

Lines 3–6: The story of Tobias and the archangel Raphael is told in Tobit, a book among the biblical Apocrypha. Tobias's father sends him on a journey to collect a debt, and he eventually meets the angel, who brings his errand to a successful conclusion.

Die dritte Elegie

Eines ist, die Geliebte zu singen. Ein anderes, wehe,
jenen verborgenen schuldigen Fluß-Gott des Bluts.
Den sie von weitem erkennt, ihren Jüngling, was weiß er
selbst von dem Herren der Lust, der aus dem Einsamen oft,
ehe das Mädchen noch linderte, oft auch als wäre sie nicht,
ach, von welchem Unkenntlichen triefend, das Gotthaupt
aufhob, aufrufend die Nacht zu unendlichem Aufruhr.
O des Blutes Neptun, o sein furchtbarer Dreizack,
o der dunkele Wind seiner Brust aus gewundener Muschel.
Horch, wie die Nacht sich muldet und höhlt. Ihr Sterne,
stammt nicht von euch des Liebenden Lust zu dem Antlitz
seiner Geliebten? Hat er die innige Einsicht
in ihr reines Gesicht nicht aus dem reinen Gestirn?

Du nicht hast ihm, wehe, nicht seine Mutter
hat ihm die Bogen der Braun so zur Erwartung gespannt.
Nicht an dir, ihn fühlendes Mädchen, an dir nicht
bog seine Lippe sich zum fruchtbarern Ausdruck.
Meinst du wirklich, ihn hätte dein leichter Auftritt
also erschüttert, du, die wandelt wie Frühwind?
Zwar du erschrakst ihm das Herz; doch ältere Schrecken
stürzten in ihn bei dem berührenden Anstoß.
Ruf ihn ... du rufst ihn nicht ganz aus dunkelem Umgang.
Freilich, er *will*, er entspringt; erleichtert gewöhnt er
sich in dein heimliches Herz und nimmt und beginnt sich.

The Third Elegy

To sing of the beloved is one thing. Ah, but of the hidden,
culpable river-god that our blood is, quite another.
Her young man, the one she doesn't quite grasp, what can even
he know about the Lord of Desire? At times, as someone alone,
and before his beloved could soothe him—indeed, as though
she didn't exist—he thrust up the godhead, dripping
with the unknowable, and roused the night to unending tumult.
Oh, Neptune in our blood, that frightening trident he holds,
his lungs' dark blasts sent through the spiral conch shell. See
how night enfolds and hollows itself out. Stars overhead,
doesn't a lover's desire for the beloved's countenance
descend from you? Did he not get his inward sense
of her features' purity from the purest of heavenly bodies?

It was neither you, alas, nor his mother who stretched
the bow of his brow toward any such expectation.
Not for you, young devotee of his, for you his mouth never
stretched open to attain a richer expressiveness.
Did you really imagine that your soft steps would make him
                                        tremble
so much, you who stroll about as lightly as the dawn wind?
True, you stirred up fear in his heart, but terrors still older
pounced on him at your first rousing contact. Go on, call him!
But you won't quite summon him away from his dubious
                                        company.
Certainly, he'd *like* to elude it, and does; unburdened, he settles
                                        down
in your warm, familiar heart. And takes himself to his
                                        initiation.

Aber begann er sich je?
Mutter, *du* machtest ihn klein, du warsts, die ihn anfing;
dir war er neu, du beugtest über die neuen
Augen die freundliche Welt und wehrtest der fremden.
Wo, ach, hin sind die Jahre, da du ihm einfach
mit der schlanken Gestalt wallendes Chaos vertratst?
Vieles verbargst du ihm so; das nächtlich-verdächtige Zimmer
machtest du harmlos, aus deinem Herzen voll Zuflucht
mischtest du menschlichern Raum seinem Nacht-Raum hinzu.
Nicht in die Finsternis, nein, in dein näheres Dasein
hast du das Nachtlicht gestellt, und es schien wie aus

                                        Freundschaft.
Nirgends ein Knistern, das du nicht lächelnd erklärtest,
so als wüßtest du längst, *wann* sich die Diele benimmt . . .
Und er horchte und linderte sich. So vieles vermochte
zärtlich dein Aufstehn; hinter den Schrank trat
hoch im Mantel sein Schicksal, und in die Falten des Vorhangs
paßte, die leicht sich verschob, seine unruhige Zukunft.

Und er selbst, wie er lag, der Erleichterte, unter
schläfernden Lidern deiner leichten Gestaltung
Süße lösend in den gekosteten Vorschlaf -:
schien ein Gehüteter . . . Aber *innen*: wer wehrte,
hinderte innen in ihm die Fluten der Herkunft?
Ach, da *war* keine Vorsicht im Schlafenden; schlafend,
aber träumend, aber in Fiebern: wie er sich ein-ließ.
Er, der Neue, Scheuende, wie er verstrickt war,
mit des innern Geschehens weiterschlagenden Ranken
schon zu Mustern verschlungen, zu würgendem Wachstum, zu

                                        tierhaft

But did he ever begin on his own?
Mother, *you* made him your little one, you began him;
he was something new, and you let a friendly world bend

                                     towards

those new eyes of his just as you fended off anything alien.
But where have they gone, the years when you simply
let your slender figure obstruct the onrush of chaos?
You hid so much from him; what he found menacing in his room
at night, you rendered harmless; out of your heart's ample refuge
you stirred a more human ambient into his nighttime realm.
Not in the darkness did you set the night-light, no, but within
your own more intimate being, where it shone like a kindly deed.
Never a creak that you failed to account for with a smile, as if
you'd long ago known just when the floorboard would behave

                                   that way . . .

So he listened and felt relief. You managed to do so much just
by quietly getting up when he called. Wrapped in a cape, his high
destiny withdrew behind the armoire, and the turbulent future,
gently shifting, fit itself into the folds of the curtain.

As for him, how he would rest there, soothed, and under his

                                   sleepy

eyelids the sweetness of your soft embodiment of things
would melt into the sips of drowsiness he tasted—: he did seem
to be someone who was protected . . . Inwardly, though, who
defended him, who inside him held off the welter of origins?
Alas, he took no precautions while sleeping, a sleeper,
but also a dreamer, who, overtaken by fever, sank down into it.
A novice and skittish, how entangled he became in interiority's
expanding onslaught of vines, which knotted themselves in

                                   patterns,

in strangling growths, in predatory animal

jagenden Formen. Wie er sich hingab -. Liebte.
Liebte sein Inneres, seines Inneren Wildnis,
diesen Urwald in ihm, auf dessen stummem Gestürztsein
lichtgrün sein Herz stand. Liebte. Verließ es, ging die
eigenen Wurzeln hinaus in gewaltigen Ursprung,
wo seine kleine Geburt schon überlebt war. Liebend
stieg er hinab in das ältere Blut, in die Schluchten,
wo das Furchtbare lag, noch satt von den Vätern. Und jedes
Schreckliche kannte ihn, blinzelte, war wie verständigt.
Ja, das Entsetzliche lächelte . . . Selten
hast du so zärtlich gelächelt, Mutter. Wie sollte
er es nicht lieben, da es ihm lächelte. *Vor* dir
hat ers geliebt, denn, da du ihn trugst schon,
war es im Wasser gelöst, das den Keimenden leicht macht.

Siehe, wir lieben nicht, wie die Blumen, aus einem
einzigen Jahr; uns steigt, wo wir lieben,
unvordenklicher Saft in die Arme. O Mädchen,
dies: daß wir liebten *in* uns, nicht Eines, ein Künftiges, sondern
das zahllos Brauende; nicht ein einzelnes Kind,
sondern die Väter, die wie Trümmer Gebirgs
uns im Grunde beruhn; sondern das trockene Flußbett
einstiger Mütter -; sondern die ganze
lautlose Landschaft unter dem wolkigen oder
reinen Verhängnis -: *dies* kam dir, Mädchen, zuvor.

Und du selber, was weißt du -, du locktest
Vorzeit empor in dem Liebenden. Welche Gefühle
wühlten herauf aus entwandelten Wesen. Welche
Frauen haßten dich da. Was für finstere Männer
regtest du auf im Geäder des Jünglings? Tote

shapes. How he gave himself over to it—. Loved.
Loved his inwardness, the wilderness within,
that primeval forest inside him, on whose silent wreckage
his pale green heart stood. Loved. Left it, went out
through his own roots in a powerful genesis
where his minor birth was already a bygone. Lovingly,
he climbed down into a more ancient blood, into ravines
where Horror lay, still gorged with the forefathers. And each
Terror knew him, gave him a conspiratorial wink.
Yes, Atrocity smiled . . . Seldom
did you, Mother, smile as tenderly. Why should
he not love it, since it smiled at him. Even before you
that was his first love, because, as you carried him,
it suffused the waters floating the embryo.

Look, we don't love like flowers that last only
a single year; when we love, a primordial sap
rises into our limbs. Young girl, there is this:
in ourselves, we love not just one imminent thing,
but instead an immeasurable ferment, not just one child by itself,
but rather our forefathers, strewn like rubble from a mountain
range
at our deepest foundation; rather, the dried-up riverbeds
that yesteryear's mothers are—, rather, the entire
voiceless landscape beneath a clouded or a shining
destiny—: all these things, dear young girl, preceded you.

And you yourself, how much do you know—you called forth
past eras in your lover. What emotions
churned their way out from beings no longer present. Which
women hated you there. Just how sinister were the men
you stirred up in your lover's youthful pulse? Deceased

Kinder wollten zu dir . . . O leise, leise,
tu ein liebes vor ihm, ein verläßliches Tagwerk, - führ ihn
nah an den Garten heran, gieb ihm der Nächte
Übergewicht . . . . . .
                    Verhalt ihn . . . . . .

children tried to reach you . . . Oh gently, gently
perform for his sake some kindly, expert task,—lead him
up close to the garden, give him more than the night's
full measure . . . . . .
                    Rein him in . . . . . .

Die vierte Elegie

O Bäume Lebens, o wann winterlich?
Wir sind nicht einig. Sind nicht wie die Zug-
vögel verständigt. Überholt und spät,
so drängen wir uns plötzlich Winden auf
und fallen ein auf teilnahmslosen Teich.
Blühn und verdorrn ist uns zugleich bewußt.
Und irgendwo gehn Löwen noch und wissen,
solang sie herrlich sind, von keiner Ohnmacht.

Uns aber, wo wir Eines meinen, ganz,
ist schon des andern Aufwand fühlbar. Feindschaft
ist uns das Nächste. Treten Liebende
nicht immerfort an Ränder, eins im andern,
die sich versprachen Weite, Jagd und Heimat.
    Da wird für eines Augenblickes Zeichnung
ein Grund von Gegenteil bereitet,
mühsam, daß wir sie sähen; denn man ist
sehr deutlich mit uns. Wir kennen den Kontur
des Fühlens nicht: nur, was ihn formt von außen.
    Wer saß nicht bang vor seines Herzens Vorhang?
Der schlug sich auf: die Szenerie war Abschied.
Leicht zu verstehen. Der bekannte Garten,
und schwankte leise: dann erst kam der Tänzer.
Nicht *der*. Genug! Und wenn er auch so leicht tut,
er ist verkleidet und er wird ein Bürger
und geht durch seine Küche in die Wohnung.
    Ich will nicht diese halbgefüllten Masken,
lieber die Puppe. Die ist voll. Ich will
den Balg aushalten und den Draht und ihr

The Fourth Elegy

O Trees of Life, speak, when do things turn wintry?
We're not at one. And don't have, like migrating
birds, an innate grasp of things. Outdone,
belated, we toss ourselves to the winds,
then fall to some disinterested pond.
Flowering and fading come to consciousness
in the same instant. Elsewhere, lions pace,
unaware, while they're kings, of any weakness.

We, though, even when intent on one thing,
foresee the attention other things will need.
Conflict's our close companion. Lovers: don't they
always hit fences in each other? Despite
the promise of open spaces, hunting, home comforts.
　　　Even for sketches done in the wink of an eye,
a contrasting background is prepared with skill
so that we might see clearly; we're meant to grasp
what's depicted. We never know the contour
of feeling, only what shapes it from the outside.
　　　Who hasn't waited in fear before his heart's
curtain? Which opened on the Farewell Scene.
Easy to understand. The routine garden,
stirring a little. Then the dancer entered.
Not *him*! Enough! No matter how light his step,
he's a disguised suburbanite, a man
who uses the back door to enter his house.
　　　No, I will *not* have these half-empty masks,
but instead, a puppet. Which is at least packed full.
I'd rather deal with its shell, its wires, that face

Gesicht und Aussehn. Hier. Ich bin davor.
Wenn auch die Lampen ausgehn, wenn mir auch
gesagt wird: Nichts mehr -, wenn auch von der Bühne
das Leere herkommt mit dem grauen Luftzug,
wenn auch von meinen stillen Vorfahrn keiner
mehr mit mir dasitzt, keine Frau, sogar
der Knabe nicht mehr mit dem braunen Schielaug:
Ich bleibe dennoch. Es giebt immer Zuschaun.

Hab ich nicht recht? Du, der um mich so bitter
das Leben schmeckte, meines kostend, Vater,
den ersten trüben Aufguß meines Müssens,
da ich heranwuchs, immer wieder kostend
und, mit dem Nachgeschmack so fremder Zukunft
beschäftigt, prüftest mein beschlagnes Aufschaun, -
der du, mein Vater, seit du tot bist, oft
in meiner Hoffnung, innen in mir, Angst hast,
und Gleichmut, wie ihn Tote haben, Reiche
von Gleichmut, aufgiebst für mein bißchen Schicksal,
hab ich nicht recht? Und ihr, hab ich nicht recht,
die ihr mich liebtet für den kleinen Anfang
Liebe zu euch, von dem ich immer abkam,
weil mir der Raum in eurem Angesicht,
da ich ihn liebte, überging in Weltraum,
in dem ihr nicht mehr wart . . . . : wenn mir zumut ist,
zu warten vor der Puppenbühne, nein,
so völlig hinzuschaun, daß, um mein Schauen
am Ende aufzuwiegen, dort als Spieler
ein Engel hinmuß, der die Bälge hochreißt.
Engel und Puppe: dann ist endlich Schauspiel.
Dann kommt zusammen, was wir immerfort
entzwein, indem wir da sind. Dann entsteht

composed of mere appearance. I'm here, out front!
Even if the house lights dim, and they say,
Sorry, that's it—, even if emptiness
flows downstage towards me on a grayish breeze,
and no silent ancestor of mine remains
sitting beside me, no housewife, nor even
that boy whose brown eyes used to squint: I still
won't rise. There is some watching left to do.

Am I not right? You, Father, you whose life
with me turned bitter after you had sampled
that early, turbid infusion of my demands;
who went on, as I grew, to sip more samples,
and, troubled by the aftertaste of so
alien a future, searched my clouded gaze,—
which you, dear Father, continue since your death
to ponder, there inside my inmost hopes.
You've renounced that peace accorded to the dead,
the peaceable kingdom itself, for my meager fate,
am I not right? And right about all of you who loved me
at the first signs of love I showed? Which I
foreswore because the compass of your faces,
as I loved them, expanded into cosmos,
with you no longer there . . . Am I not allowed
to sit and wait before the puppet stage, or
stare at it so hard that a performing
angel must then come and counteract
my gaze by jerking the packed forms awake?
Angel and puppet: theatre at last.
Then comes a union that we always sunder
simply by being present. From the seasons of

aus unsern Jahreszeiten erst der Umkreis
des ganzen Wandelns. Über uns hinüber
spielt dann der Engel. Sieh, die Sterbenden,
sollten sie nicht vermuten, wie voll Vorwand
das alles ist, was wir hier leisten. Alles
ist nicht es selbst. O Stunden in der Kindheit,
da hinter den Figuren mehr als nur
Vergangnes war und vor uns nicht die Zukunft.
Wir wuchsen freilich und wir drängten manchmal,
bald groß zu werden, denen halb zulieb,
die andres nicht mehr hatten, als das Großsein.
Und waren doch, in unserem Alleingehn,
mit Dauerndem vergnügt und standen da
im Zwischenraume zwischen Welt und Spielzeug,
an einer Stelle, die seit Anbeginn
gegründet war für einen reinen Vorgang.

Wer zeigt ein Kind, so wie es steht? Wer stellt
es ins Gestirn und giebt das Maß des Abstands
ihm in die Hand? Wer macht den Kindertod
aus grauem Brot, das hart wird, - oder läßt
ihn drin im runden Mund, so wie den Gröps
von einem schönen Apfel? . . . . Mörder sind
leicht einzusehen. Aber dies: den Tod,
den ganzen Tod, noch *vor* dem Leben so
sanft zu enthalten und nicht bös zu sein,
ist unbeschreiblich.

our lives, the whole of it arises, a cycle
of transformation. Then, above, beyond us,
an angel is performing. Look at the dying:
won't they guess how much contrivance went
into the task that we accomplish here?
All is not just itself. Oh, childhood hours,
when behind those figures there was more
than mere time past, and before us, not mere future.
We developed, certainly, and often strove
to grow up faster, half to humor people
who, though adult, had nothing else to give.
And yet we, in our solitary way,
were content with things that lasted, and we stood there
in the no-man's-land dividing world and toy,
a place that from the earliest beginning
had been established for an outcome wholly pure.

Who shows a child just as he is? Installs him
among the stars or puts the measuring-rod
of distance in his hands? Who makes a childhood
death out of dull gray bread that then turns hard,—
or leaves it there, the core of a ripe apple
in an opened mouth? . . . Oh, murderers are easy
to fathom. But consider: to encompass
death gently, death beheld entire, before
you've lived at all, and still not feel resentment:
that's inexpressible.

Die fünfte Elegie

FRAU HERTHA KOENIG ZUGEEIGNET

Wer aber *sind* sie, sag mir, die Fahrenden, diese ein wenig
Flüchtigern noch als wir selbst, die dringend von früh an
wringt ein *wem, wem* zu Liebe
niemals zufriedener Wille? Sondern er wringt sie,
biegt sie, schlingt sie und schwingt sie,
wirft sie und fängt sie zurück; wie aus geölter,
glatterer Luft kommen sie nieder
auf dem verzehrten, von ihrem ewigen
Aufsprung dünneren Teppich, diesem verlorenen
Teppich im Weltall.
Aufgelegt wie ein Pflaster, als hätte der Vorstadt-
Himmel der Erde dort wehe getan.
                    Und kaum dort,
aufrecht, da und gezeigt: des Dastehns
großer Anfangsbuchstab . . ., schon auch, die stärksten
Männer, rollt sie wieder, zum Scherz, der immer
kommende Griff, wie August der Starke bei Tisch
einen zinnenen Teller.

Ach und um diese
Mitte, die Rose des Zuschauns:
blüht und entblättert. Um diesen
Stampfer, den Stempel, den von dem eignen
blühenden Staub getroffnen, zur Scheinfrucht
wieder der Unlust befrucheten, ihrer

The Fifth Elegy

DEDICATED TO FRAU HERTHA KOENIG

Tell me who they might be, these transients, a touch more
fly-by-night even than ourselves, troupers who early on
get stung by, wrung by, a will (*whose* will? for whose *sake?*)
that never seems satisfied. Instead, it wrings them,
bends, loops, and swings them, flings
and catches them up again; as if, through an air
oiled for greater smoothness, they land
on a worn-out carpet, made still more threadbare
by their eternal leaping up: a scrap of carpet
now lost in the great sum of things,
laid down like a bandage, as though skies
over the city's outskirts had wounded the ground.
            And no sooner do they pose—
upright, on display, Doggedness's outsized
initial **D**—than the strongest are just for fun rolled up again
by a grip as relentless as Augustus the Strong's, who once
at table did the same to a pewter plate.

Yes, and around this
center onlookers form a rose:
which blooms and lets fall its petals. Around this
piston, this pistil, brushed by its own
pollen and again made to produce
the wax fruit of tedium, never

niemals bewußten, - glänzend mit dünnster
Oberfläche leicht scheinlächelnden Unlust.

Da: der welke, faltige Stemmer,
der alte, der nur noch trommelt,
eingegangen in seiner gewaltigen Haut, als hätte sie früher
zwei Männer enthalten, und einer
läge nun schon auf dem Kirchhof, und er überlebte den andern,
taub und manchmal ein wenig
wirr, in der verwitweten Haut.

Aber der junge, der Mann, als wär er der Sohn eines Nackens
und einer Nonne: prall und strammig erfüllt
mit Muskeln und Einfalt.

Oh ihr,
die ein Leid, das noch klein war,
einst als Spielzeug bekam, in einer seiner
langen Genesungen . . . .

Du, der mit dem Aufschlag,
wie nur Früchte ihn kennen, unreif,
täglich hundertmal abfällt vom Baum der gemeinsam
erbauten Bewegung (der, rascher als Wasser, in wenig
Minuten Lenz, Sommer und Herbst hat) -
abfällt und anprallt ans Grab:
manchmal, in halber Pause, will dir ein liebes
Antlitz entstehn hinüber zu deiner selten
zärtlichen Mutter; doch an deinen Körper verliert sich,
der es flächig verbraucht, das schüchtern
kaum versuchte Gesicht . . . Und wieder

acknowledged by it,—a tedium gleaming
with the thinnest overlay of fake, weightless smiles.

Look: the sagging, wrinkled strongman,
the oldster who nowadays only beats the drum,
shrunken away in his tough hide, as though it had earlier
contained *two* men, one of them
already asleep in the graveyard, survived meanwhile by the other,
deaf and often a little
confused in his widower's skin.

But the younger one, his successor, looks like the hybrid
of a neck and a nun: stalwart, yes, pumped up
with muscles and naïveté.

Oh all of you there, given
like presents to Sorrow (back when it was still little),
a toy to play with during one
of its long convalescences . . .

And then there's you, as yet unripe, who,
with the sort of thud that only dropped fruit makes,
fall every day a hundred times from the tree of jointly
constructed routines (faster than water, in a few
moments it passes through spring, summer and autumn)—
you plummet and crash on the grave:
sometimes, in an instant, a loving look
will grow from within all the way to a mother
seldom kind to you; yet it thins out over your body,
whose surface leaches away that shy,
barely attempted expression . . . and again

klatscht der Mann in die Hand zu dem Ansprung, und eh dir
jemals ein Schmerz deutlicher wird in der Nähe des immer
trabenden Herzens, kommt das Brennen der Fußsohln
ihm, seinem Ursprung, zuvor mit ein paar dir
rasch in die Augen gejagten leiblichen Tränen.
Und dennoch, blindlings,
das Lächeln . . . . .

Engel! o nimms, pflücks, das kleinblütige Heilkraut.
Schaff eine Vase, verwahrs! Stells unter jene, uns *noch* nicht
offenen Freuden; in lieblicher Urne
rühms mit blumiger schwungiger Aufschrift: >*Subrisio Saltat.*<.

Du dann, Liebliche,
du, von den reizendsten Freuden
stumm Übersprungne. Vielleicht sind
deine Fransen glücklich für dich -,
oder über den jungen
prallen Brüsten die grüne metallene Seide
fühlt sich unendlich verwöhnt und entbehrt nichts.
Du,
immerfort anders auf alle des Gleichgewichts schwankende
                                                   Waagen
hingelegte Marktfrucht des Gleichmuts,
öffentlich unter den Schultern.

Wo, o *wo* ist der Ort - ich trag ihn im Herzen -,
wo sie noch lange nicht *konnten*, noch voneinander
abfieln, wie sich bespringende, nicht recht
paarige Tiere; -
wo die Gewichte noch schwer sind;

the man claps his hands for your leap, and before
pain comes into sharp focus close to your constantly
racing heart, a burning sensation in your foot-soles
outruns that first ache, and a few palpable tears
get hurried right into your eyes.
Nevertheless, in all blindness,
that smile . . . . .

Angel! Oh take it, gather that small-blossomed heal-all.
Get a vase to keep it in! Put it among those joys *still* not
available to us. In a lovely urn acclaim,
and with a lavish flourish inscribe on it: *Subrisio Saltat.*

And then you, lovely thing,
you, the one silently leapt over
by the most magical joys. Maybe your fringed hems
do the job of feeling your happiness for you—,
or else the green, metallic silk
covering your firm young breasts considers
itself altogether indulged, and lacks for nothing.
You,
constantly shifted on the balancing trays of the scale,
indifference's vended fruit put on display,
exhibited among men's shoulders.

Oh *where* is that place now—I keep it in my heart—
where they still weren't very skillful, still broke
apart like poorly matched animals
trying to mate with each other;—
the place where barbells are still heavy,

wo noch von ihren vergeblich
wirbelnden Stäben die Teller
torkeln . . . . .

Und plötzlich in diesem mühsamen Nirgends, plötzlich
die unsägliche Stelle, wo sich das reine Zuwenig
unbegreiflich verwandelt -, umspringt
in jenes leere Zuviel.
Wo die vielstellige Rechnung
zahlenlos aufgeht.

Plätze, o Platz in Paris, unendlicher Schauplatz,
wo die Modistin, *Madame Lamort*,
die ruhlosen Wege der Erde, endlose Bänder,
schlingt und windet und neue aus ihnen
Schleifen erfindet, Rüschen, Blumen, Kokarden, künstliche
    Früchte -, alle
unwahr gefärbt, - für die billigen
Winterhüte des Schicksals.
. . . .

Engel!: Es wäre ein Platz, den wir nicht wissen, und dorten,
auf unsäglichem Teppich, zeigten die Liebenden, die's hier
bis zum Können nie bringen, ihre kühnen
hohen Figuren des Herzschwungs,
ihre Türme aus Lust, ihre
längst, wo Boden nie war, nur an einander
lehnenden Leitern, bebend, - und *könntens*,
vor den Zuschauern rings, unzähligen lautlosen Toten:
    Würfen die dann ihre letzten, immer ersparten,

where plates on pointlessly
turning batons still do
spin around . . . . .

And suddenly in this burdensome Nowhere, suddenly
the ineffable place, where pure Scarcity
is mysteriously transfigured,—and whirls about
into an empty Surfeit.
Where the computation with multiple digits
is solved and with no remainder.

Squares. O Paris square, eternal showcase
where the milliner Madame Lamort
loops and winds those endless ribbons, anxious
roadways of the earth, and from them invents
new bows, ruffs, flowers, cockades, artificial fruits—, all
dyed improbable colors,—for the cheap
winter bonnets donned by Fate.
. . . .

Angel! If there were a square we didn't know of, a place where,
on a mysterious carpet, lovers might perform all they'd never
managed to master on earth, their bold, high-flying
patterns for leaps the heart made across space, towers
built of pleasure,
ladders set up on no foundation, for a long time
trembling and leaning only on each other,—and *could*
master it all for the circle of spectators, the numberless,
                                        voiceless dead:
    Wouldn't that crowd now toss their last coins—ever
                                        saved up,

immer verborgenen, die wir nicht kennen, ewig
gültigen Münzen des Glücks vor das endlich
wahrhaft lächelnde Paar auf gestilltem
Teppich?

ever hidden away and unknown to us, this eternally
valid currency of happiness—towards
the couple at last truthfully smiling there on the requited
carpet?

Notes

Hertha Koenig (1884–1976), Rilke's friend, a German writer and art collector who on Rilke's advice bought Picasso's *La Famille des saltimbanques* (*The Acrobat Family*, 1905). In the summer of 1915, Rilke stayed in her Munich apartment, where the painting was hung. It is a source for the imagery of this Elegy.

initial **D**: In Picasso's painting, the grouping of the acrobats could be seen as suggesting the outline of an uppercase letter D. Or else Rilke imagines them in their various interactive poses as forming the letter D. In the text the German noun "Dastehen" ("standing-thereness" or "endurance") begins, like all nouns in German, with an uppercase letter. It would be thrown into even sharper relief as an enlarged initial for texts printed in the German typeface known as *Fraktur* ("black letter": see the Gothic typeface used for the name of *The New York Times*). The D-shape I convey using the word "Doggedness," to suggest the acrobats' will to endure.

Augustus the Strong: Frederick Augustus I (1670–1733), Elector of Saxony and later King of Poland. Known as "the Strong" because of feats like the one Rilke mentions.

Subrisio Saltat: Or, written out completely, *subrisio saltatorum*, meaning "the smile of the tumblers" (or "acrobats"). Rilke writes it in abbreviated form, the way it might appear on a label affixed to the urn he imagines.

Die sechste Elegie

Feigenbaum, seit wie lange schon ists mir bedeutend,
wie du die Blüte beinah ganz überschlägst
und hinein in die zeitig entschlossene Frucht,
ungerühmt, drängst dein reines Geheimnis.
Wie der Fontäne Rohr treibt dein gebognes Gezweig
abwärts den Saft und hinan: und er springt aus dem Schlaf,
fast nicht erwachend, ins Glück seiner süßesten Leistung.
Sieh: wie der Gott in den Schwan.

      . . . . . . Wir aber verweilen,
ach, uns rühmt es zu blühn, und ins verspätete Innre
unserer endlichen Frucht gehn wir verraten hinein.
Wenigen steigt so stark der Andrang des Handelns,
daß sie schon anstehn und glühn in der Fülle des Herzens,
wenn die Verführung zum Blühn wie gelinderte Nachtluft
ihnen die Jugend des Munds, ihnen die Lider berührt:
Helden vielleicht und den frühe Hinüberbestimmten,
denen der gärtnernde Tod anders die Adern verbiegt.
Diese stürzen dahin: dem eigenen Lächeln
sind sie voran, wie das Rossegespann in den milden
muldigen Bildern von Karnak dem siegenden König.

Wunderlich nah ist der Held doch den jugendlich Toten.

                                          Dauern
ficht ihn nicht an. Sein Aufgang ist Dasein; beständig
nimmt er sich fort und tritt ins veränderte Sternbild
seiner steten Gefahr. Dort fänden ihn wenige. Aber,
das uns finster verschweigt, das plötzlich begeisterte Schicksal
singt ihn hinein in den Sturm seiner aufrauschenden Welt.

The Sixth Elegy

Fig-tree, for a long time it's had meaning for me,
the way you almost entirely get round your flowering
and, with no pretension, urge your pristine secrecy
into a fruit that early on takes a determined form.
Much like a fountain spout, your arching boughs drive
the sap downward and onward; it wells up from dormancy,
not yet fully alert, into the triumph of its sweetest triumph.
Behold: the god transformed into a swan.

      . . . . . . We, though, dawdle,
basking in the renown flowering confers, and, compromised,
enter the slow-to-ripen insides of our eventual fruit.
Only a few feel the push toward action so strongly
as to stop short, glowing with heartfelt plenitude
when the inducement to blossom, like softened evening air,
touches their youthful mouths and brushes their eyelids:
heroes maybe, and those marked for early migration, whose veins
have been differently espaliered by the gardener Death.
A length ahead of their own smiles they plunge,
like a team of chargers advancing before the victor king
in those mild sunken-relief carvings of Karnak.

Uncanny how closely the hero resembles the early dead. Putting
down roots doesn't interest him. Ascent is his true dwelling; he
                      always
pulls himself away and steps into the shifting constellation
of chronic danger. Not many could find him there. But
Fate, to us obscure and silent, is suddenly quickened
and sings him into the storm of a world in upheaval.

Hör ich doch keinen wie *ihn*. Auf einmal durchgeht mich
mit der strömenden Luft sein verdunkelter Ton.

Dann, wie verbärg ich mich gern vor der Sehnsucht: O wär ich,
wär ich ein Knabe und dürft es noch werden und säße
in die künftigen Arme gestützt und läse von Simson,
wie seine Mutter erst nichts und dann alles gebar.

War er nicht Held schon in dir, o Mutter, begann nicht
dort schon, in dir, seine herrische Auswahl?
Tausende brauten im Schooß und wollten er sein,
aber sieh: er ergriff und ließ aus -, wählte und konnte.
Und wenn er Säulen zerstieß, so wars, da er ausbrach
aus der Welt deines Leibs in die engere Welt, wo er weiter
wählte und konnte. O Mütter der Helden, o Ursprung
reißender Ströme! Ihr Schluchten, in die sich
hoch von dem Herzrand, klagend,
schon die Mädchen gestürzt, künftig die Opfer dem Sohn.

Denn hinstürmte der Held durch Aufenthalte der Liebe,
jeder hob ihn hinaus, jeder ihn meinende Herzschlag,
abgewendet schon, stand er am Ende der Lächeln, - anders.

I don't hear anyone like *him*. In a flash it pierces me,
that darkling note of his, carried on a gust of air.

Then how I wish I could shake off this yearning: Oh if only,
if only I were a boy again, with my life still to come, if I could
sit propped on auspicious arms and read about Samson,
how his mother at first gave birth to nothing—and then to
                                         everything.

Inside you, wasn't he already heroic, new mother, hadn't
his lordly election already begun there, inside you?
Thousands of those steeping in the womb wanted to be *him*,
but see: he gripped, and pushed aside—, chose; succeeded.
And if ever he smashed pillars into rubble, it was when he broke
                                         forth
from your body's world into a narrower one, where he could
further choose and succeed. O mothers of heroes, O source
of roiling rivers! You chasms into which,
from high up on the heart's cliff-edge, grieving young women
threw themselves down, from now forward a sacrifice to the son.

Thus if the hero stormed through love's way-stations,
each one thrust him up and onward, each heartbeat intent on him,
till, his back already turned, he stood there where smiling
                              ends,—someone else.

Die siebente Elegie

Werbung nicht mehr, nicht Werbung, entwachsene Stimme,
sei deines Schreies Natur; zwar schrieest du rein wie der Vogel,
wenn ihn die Jahreszeit aufhebt, die steigende, beinah
                                                vergessend,
daß er ein kümmerndes Tier und nicht nur ein einzelnes Herz
                                                      sei,
das sie ins Heitere wirft, in die innigen Himmel. Wie er, so
würbest du wohl, nicht minder -, daß, noch unsichtbar,
dich die Freundin erführ, die stille, in der eine Antwort
langsam erwacht und über dem Hören sich anwärmt, -
deinem erkühnten Gefühl die erglühte Gefühlin.

O und der Frühling begriffe -, da ist keine Stelle,
die nicht trüge den Ton der Verkündigung. Erst jenen kleinen
fragenden Auflaut, den, mit steigernder Stille,
weithin umschweigt ein reiner bejahender Tag.
Dann die Stufen hinan, Ruf-Stufen hinan, zum geträumten
Tempel der Zukunft -; dann den Triller, Fontäne,
die zu dem drängenden Strahl schon das Fallen zuvornimmt
im versprechlichen Spiel . . . . Und vor sich, den Sommer.

Nicht nur die Morgen alle des Sommers -, nicht nur
wie sie sich wandeln in Tag und strahlen vor Anfang.
Nicht nur die Tage, die zart sind um Blumen, und oben,
um die gestalteten Bäume, stark und gewaltig.
Nicht nur die Andacht dieser entfalteten Kräfte,
nicht nur die Wege, nicht nur die Wiesen im Abend,
nicht nur, nach spätem Gewitter, das atmende Klarsein,
nicht nur der nahende Schlaf und ein Ahnen, abends . . .

The Seventh Elegy

Pandering: no more of that, Voice. An approach you've now
                                        outgrown
shouldn't prompt your song, even if you cried out cleanly as a bird
when the season in its ascent thrusts him aloft and almost forgets
that he's wildlife, anxious, and not just a heart singled out
to be flung into the brighter skies of an inward Heaven. Like him,
you'd still be courting some beloved not yet in sight,
so that she'd take note of you, this silent person in whom a
                                        response
slowly awakens, warmed by the act of listening,—
to your enkindled feelings a responder ardent and heartfelt.

Oh, and springtime would join in too—, for there is no place
that wouldn't resound with annunciation. First, those small,
inquiring grace notes, which pure, affirmative daylight
enfolds far and wide in heightening silence.
To scale a flight of birdcall stairs, up to the dreamt-of
Temple of the Future—; then on to the trill, a fountain
whose upward-striving brilliance embraces its own falling
in playful anticipation . . . . With summer soon to come.

Not just all the summer dawns—, not just
how they mutate into day and glow with inception.
Not just the days, which, tenderly lighting the flowers, up above
grow vast and mighty among full-grown treetops.
Not just the devotion of these developing powers,
not just the pathways, the evening meadows, not just
the breathing clarity that follows late-afternoon thunderstorms,
not just approaching sleep and a sunset premonition . . .

sondern die Nächte! Sondern die hohen, des Sommers,
Nächte, sondern die Sterne, die Sterne der Erde.
O einst tot sein und sie wissen unendlich,
alle die Sterne: denn wie, wie, wie sie vergessen!

Siehe, da rief ich die Liebende. Aber nicht *sie* nur
käme . . . Es kämen aus schwächlichen Gräbern
Mädchen und ständen . . . Denn wie beschränk ich,
wie, den gerufenen Ruf? Die Versunkenen suchen
immer noch Erde. - Ihr Kinder, ein hiesig
einmal ergriffenes Ding gälte für viele.
Glaubt nicht, Schicksal sei mehr, als das Dichte der Kindheit;
wie überholtet ihr oft den Geliebten, atmend,
atmend nach seligem Lauf, auf nichts zu, ins Freie.

Hiersein ist herrlich. Ihr wußtet es, Mädchen, *ihr* auch,
die ihr scheinbar entbehrtet, versankt -, ihr, in den ärgsten
Gassen der Städte, Schwärende, oder dem Abfall
Offene. Denn eine Stunde war jeder, vielleicht nicht
ganz eine Stunde, ein mit den Maßen der Zeit kaum
Meßliches zwischen zwei Weilen -, da sie ein Dasein
hatte. Alles. Die Adern voll Dasein.
Nur, wir vergessen so leicht, was der lachende Nachbar
uns nicht bestätigt oder beneidet. Sichtbar
wollen wirs heben, wo doch das sichtbarste Glück uns
erst zu erkennen sich giebt, wenn wir es innen verwandeln.

Nirgends, Geliebte, wird Welt sein, als innen. Unser
Leben geht hin mit Verwandlung. Und immer geringer
schwindet das Außen. Wo einmal ein dauerndes Haus war,

but instead, the nights! Instead, summer's exalted
nights, instead, stars, our earth's own stars.
Oh, to have died at last, to know them forever, all the stars,
for how, tell me, how can one forget them!

So, you see, I called to my beloved. But not only that one person
came . . . Out of weakening graves, other young women
would come and foregather . . . For, the call once sent forth,
how could I restrict its reach? Those who've foundered and are
                                                    sinking
always try to get back to land.—Children, hear me: one solid
thing, when it's firmly grasped, will amount to many others.
Do not value Fate more than the richness of childhood.
For how often you outdistanced your beloved, panting, panting
after the blissful sprint, towards nothingness, into the clear.

Just being here is glorious. Even you knew that, young girls
who must have suffered want, and went under—in the sordid
back-alleys of the city, festering or filling up with debris
others had tossed away. You each got an hour, perhaps not even
a full hour, between two sessions, a timespan barely
measurable at all, when you could live and simply
be there. All of it. Your arteries pulsing with existence.
Yet we soon dismiss what we have if our mocking neighbor
neither notices or covets it. We seem bent
on holding it up to view, but not even joy at its most manifest
lets itself be known until we've transfigured it with inwardness.

Nowhere, love, will the world abide save in inwardness. Our life
moves onward in transfiguration. And steadily smaller shrinks
the ambit of the merely external. Where once an enduring
                                                    house was,

schlägt sich erdachtes Gebild vor, quer, zu Erdenklichem
völlig gehörig, als ständ es noch ganz im Gehirne.
Weite Speicher der Kraft schafft sich der Zeitgeist, gestaltlos
wie der spannende Drang, den er aus allem gewinnt.
Tempel kennt er nicht mehr. Diese, des Herzens,
                                        Verschwendung
sparen wir heimlicher ein. Ja, wo noch eins übersteht,
ein einst gebetetes Ding, ein gedientes, geknietes -,
hält es sich, so wie es ist, schon ins Unsichtbare hin.
Viele gewahrens nicht mehr, doch ohne den Vorteil,
daß sie's nun *innerlich* baun, mit Pfeilern und Statuen, größer!

Jede dumpfe Umkehr der Welt hat solche Enterbte,
denen das Frühere nicht und noch nicht das Nächste gehört.
Denn auch das Nächste ist weit für die Menschen. *Uns* soll
dies nicht verwirren; es stärke in uns die Bewahrung
der noch erkannten Gestalt. - Dies *stand* einmal unter
                                        Menschen,
mitten im Schicksal stands, im vernichtenden, mitten
im Nichtwissen-Wohin stand es, wie seiend, und bog
Sterne zu sich aus gesicherten Himmeln. Engel,
dir noch zeig ich es, *da*! in deinem Anschaun
steht es gerettet zuletzt, nun endlich aufrecht.
Säulen, Pylone, der Sphinx, das strebende Stemmen,
grau aus vergehender Stadt oder aus fremder, des Doms.

War es nicht Wunder? O staune, Engel, denn *wir* sinds,
wir, o du Großer, erzähls, daß wir solches vermochten, mein Atem
reicht für die Rühmung nicht aus. So haben wir dennoch
nicht die Räume versäumt, diese gewährenden, diese
unseren Räume. (Was müssen sie fürchterlich groß sein,

an image passes before the mind's eye, fully domesticated
to consciousness as though it had always dwelt in the brain.
The spirit of the times builds up immense reserves of power,
abstract as the driving force it captures from all that is.
Temples no longer matter to it. These extravagances our hearts
once paid for, we're spared from, in private. Yes, wherever one still
remains, a Something once prayed to, waited on, knelt before—,
that object hands itself over, just as it is, to the invisible.
Many no longer notice it, indeed, don't see the advantage
gained by building it *inwardly*, with columns and statues, grander!

With each stale turn of the world, the disinherited increase,
                                                            those
who possess neither what once was nor what is to come.
For even the next moment is far beyond humans. To *us*
it shouldn't be a quandary; let it grow stronger as we protect
a plan we still recognize.—This once stood firm among us,
stood at the core of annihilating fate; in the midst of our
motion towards we don't know what, it stood, almost real, and
                                                            bent
stars down to it out of their fixed heaven. Angel,
to *you* I still point it out: *there it is!* In your gaze
let it stand at last redeemed, now finally upright.
Pillars, pylons, the Sphinx, and the cathedral's aspiring
gray upthrust marked out against a fading or foreign city.

Wasn't it miraculous, Angel? Wonder at us and what we are,
O elevated being, say how we achieved so much, my breath
falls short when I try to praise it. So we have not after all
let these spaces go to waste, these generous spaces, which are
our own. How fearfully huge they must be if after thousands

da sie Jahrtausende nicht unseres Fühlns überfülln.)
Aber ein Turm war groß, nicht wahr? O Engel, er war es, -
groß, auch noch neben dir? Chartres war groß -, und Musik
reichte noch weiter hinan und überstieg uns. Doch selbst nur
eine Liebende -, oh, allein am nächtlichen Fenster . . . .
reichte sie dir nicht ans Knie -?

                        Glaub *nicht*, daß ich werbe.
Engel, und würb ich dich auch! Du kommst nicht. Denn mein
Anruf ist immer voll Hinweg; wider so starke
Strömung kannst du nicht schreiten. Wie ein gestreckter
Arm ist mein Rufen. Und seine zum Greifen
oben offene Hand bleibt vor dir
offen, wie Abwehr und Warnung,
Unfaßlicher, weitauf.

of years our feelings haven't filled them to overflowing.
But surely one spire was tall, may we not say? O Angel, it *was*
                                    that,—
tall, even set beside you. Chartres was great,—and music
reached up still higher and surpassed us. Yet even a woman
in love—, oh, sitting alone by night at her window . . .
did she not come up as high as your knee—?
                          Don't regard this as cajolery,
Angel; even if it were, you would not come. For my
summons is a complete holding at bay; you can't, against such
a strong current, make headway. An outstretched arm:
that's what my summoning is. And its upturned hand,
opened to grip yours, remains there before you,
open, warding off and warning
You, who can never be grasped. Wide open.

Die achte Elegie

RUDOLF KASSNER ZUGEEIGNET

Mit allen Augen sieht die Kreatur
das Offene. Nur unsre Augen sind
wie umgekehrt und ganz um sie gestellt
als Fallen, rings um ihren freien Ausgang.
Was draußen *ist*, wir wissens aus des Tiers
Antlitz allein; denn schon das frühe Kind
wenden wir um und zwingens, daß es rückwärts
Gestaltung sehe, nicht das Offne, das
im Tiergesicht so tief ist. Frei von Tod.
Ihn sehen wir allein; das freie Tier
hat seinen Untergang stets hinter sich
und vor sich Gott, und wenn es geht, so gehts
in Ewigkeit, so wie die Brunnen gehen.
    Wir haben nie, nicht einen einzigen Tag,
den reinen Raum vor uns, in den die Blumen
unendlich aufgehn. Immer ist es Welt
und niemals Nirgends ohne Nicht: das Reine,
Unüberwachte, das man atmet und
unendlich *weiß* und nicht begehrt. Als Kind
verliert sich eins im Stilln an dies und wird
gerüttelt. Oder jener stirbt und ists.
Denn nah am Tod sieht man den Tod nicht mehr
und starrt *hinaus*, vielleicht mit großem Tierblick.
Liebende, wäre nicht der andre, der
die Sicht verstellt, sind nah daran und staunen . . .

The Eighth Elegy

DEDICATED TO RUDOLF KASSNER

With all of their eyes, animals behold
openness. Only *our* seeing is
retrospective, set like traps around them,
an obstacle that blocks the path to freedom.
What *does* exist outside we come to know
from their faces alone; in fact, we make
even young children turn and take a backward
look at fixed concepts, not at the openness
deep in those mammal features. Free of death.
That, only we see; the unhindered animal
keeps its decline and sunset ever behind it,
with God before; and, if it walks, goes forward
in timelessness, like springs that well and flow.

    Yet *we* don't, not even for a single day,
have pure space before us, a place where flowers
forever bloom. It's always the real world,
never a Nowhere void of negation, a pure
Unsurveillance that can be inhaled,
forever *known* and thus not craved. As children
we lose ourselves to this in silence, until
abruptly shaken. Or someone dying *is* it,
and, near death, does not see death but stares
beyond it, his gaze perhaps large as the mammals'.
And lovers, if their partner didn't block
the view, could then draw near and be astonished . . .

Wie aus Versehn ist ihnen aufgetan
hinter dem andern . . . Aber über ihn
kommt keiner fort, und wieder wird ihm Welt.
Der Schöpfung immer zugewendet, sehn
wir nur auf ihr die Spiegelung des Frein,
von uns verdunkelt. Oder daß ein Tier,
ein stummes, aufschaut, ruhig durch uns durch.
Dieses heißt Schicksal: gegenüber sein
und nichts als das und immer gegenüber.

Wäre Bewußtheit unsrer Art in dem
sicheren Tier, das uns entgegenzieht
in anderer Richtung -, riß es uns herum
mit seinem Wandel. Doch sein Sein ist ihm
unendlich, ungefaßt und ohne Blick
auf seinen Zustand, rein, so wie sein Ausblick.
Und wo wir Zukunft sehn, dort sieht es Alles
und sich in Allem und geheilt für immer.

Und doch ist in dem wachsam warmen Tier
Gewicht und Sorge einer großen Schwermut.
Denn ihm auch haftet immer an, was uns
oft überwältigt, - die Erinnerung,
als sei schon einmal das, wonach man drängt,
näher gewesen, treuer und sein Anschluß
unendlich zärtlich. Hier ist alles Abstand,
und dort wars Atem. Nach der ersten Heimat
ist ihm die zweite zwitterig und windig.
    O Seligkeit der *kleinen* Kreatur,
die immer *bleibt* im Schooße, der sie austrug;
o Glück der Mücke, die noch *innen* hüpft,
selbst wenn sie Hochzeit hat: denn Schooß ist Alles.

As if by someone's oversight, space opens
behind the partner. Since neither can get beyond
the other, each of them turns back into World.
Forever focused on Creation, we see it
as only a mirroring of untrammeled regions
that we have darkened. Or an animal,
voiceless and calm, looks up and then straight *through* us.
Our fate consists of this: to be *against*,
nothing else but that, and *always* against.

Were consciousness like ours present in
the animal whose firm tread moves toward us
following its own guidance—, we'd be torn
along its wayward path. Its inner self, though,
is limitless, ungrasped, with no regard
for its positioning, pure, like its clear gaze.
And where we see a future, it sees All,
itself within that All, forever healed.

And yet inside the warm and watchful mammal
the weight and pain of sorrow also dwells.
For it fastens on him too, a thing that often
overpowers us,—the recognition
that what one strives so hard for was perhaps
at one time closer, truer, an alliance
endlessly tender. Here, all is detachment.
There, all was breath. And after the first home,
the next seems like mere travesty and bluster.
     O blessedness accorded the small creature
still living in the vessel where it was born.
Joy of the mayfly that leaps up *inside*
even when mating. The vessel's everything.

Und sieh die halbe Sicherheit des Vogels,
der beinah beides weiß aus seinem Ursprung,
als wär er eine Seele der Etrusker,
aus einem Toten, den ein Raum empfing,
doch mit der ruhenden Figur als Deckel.
Und wie bestürzt ist eins, das fliegen muß
und stammt aus einem Schooß. Wie vor sich selbst
erschreckt, durchzuckts die Luft, wie wenn ein Sprung
durch eine Tasse geht. So reißt die Spur
der Fledermaus durchs Porzellan des Abends.

Und wir: Zuschauer, immer, überall,
dem allen zugewandt und nie hinaus!
Uns überfüllts. Wir ordnens. Es zerfällt.
Wir ordnens wieder und zerfallen selbst.

Wer hat uns also umgedreht, daß wir,
was wir auch tun, in jener Haltung sind
von einem, welcher fortgeht? Wie er auf
dem letzten Hügel, der ihm ganz sein Tal
noch einmal zeigt, sich wendet, anhält, weilt -,
so leben wir und nehmen immer Abschied.

Observe the songbird's hindered confidence:
its hatching almost taught it to know both,
as though it were the soul of an Etruscan
whose mortal flesh an opened space received,
with his own reclining likeness as its lid.
And how it baffles those poor creatures born
from wombs, yet meant to fly. As though alarmed
at themselves they flitter through the air, much like
a crack going through a cup. So the bat's path
splits through the evening sky's porcelain.

And we, observers, relentless, everywhere,
intent on objects, never looking outside them!
They overfill us. We arrange them. They break up.
Once more we arrange. We ourselves are broken.

Then who has wheeled us backwards, so that we,
no matter the action, always seem to have
the stance of those about to depart? Like someone
on the final hill, which one more time shows him
his entire valley, who turns, pauses, lingers—,
and so we live, constantly saying farewell.

Notes

Rudolf Kassner (1873–1959), Austrian author and cultural critic, was a frequent guest at Duino, where he met and became friends with Rilke in 1907. Kassner speculated that the dedication was based on one of their conversations, during which Rilke had spoken of the "inner happiness of a gnat."

Die neunte Elegie

Warum, wenn es angeht, also die Frist des Daseins
hinzubringen, als Lorbeer, ein wenig dunkler als alles
andere Grün, mit kleinen Wellen an jedem
Blattrand (wie eines Windes Lächeln) -: warum dann
Menschliches müssen - und, Schicksal vermeidend,
sich sehnen nach Schicksal? . . .

                      Oh, *nicht*, weil Glück *ist*,
dieser voreilige Vorteil eines nahen Verlusts.
Nicht aus Neugier, oder zur Übung des Herzens,
das auch im Lorbeer *wäre* . . . . .

Aber weil Hiersein viel ist, und weil uns scheinbar
alles das Hiesige braucht, dieses Schwindende, das
seltsam uns angeht. Uns, die Schwindendsten. Ein Mal
jedes, nur *ein* Mal. *Ein* Mal und nichtmehr. Und wir auch
ein Mal. Nie wieder. Aber dieses
ein Mal gewesen zu sein, wenn auch nur *ein* Mal:
irdisch gewesen zu sein, scheint nicht widerrufbar.

Und so drängen wir uns und wollen es leisten,
wollens enthalten in unsern einfachen Händen,
im überfüllteren Blick und im sprachlosen Herzen.
Wollen es werden. - Wem es geben? Am liebsten
alles behalten für immer . . . Ach, in den andern Bezug,
wehe, was nimmt man hinüber? Nicht das Anschaun, das hier
langsam erlernte, und kein hier Ereignetes. Keins.

The Ninth Elegy

Why, since we could live the span of our entire existence
as a laurel tree, its green somewhat darker than all
the others', and each leaf deckled at the margin
with a wavelike smile like the breeze's:—why then
have to be human?—and, why do we, sidestepping
our fate, still long for that very fate? . . .

                              Oh, *not* because good fortune exists,
that precipitate gain presaging the loss to come.
Not out of curiosity, nor as an assignment given to the heart,
as if it *too* might be beating in the laurel tree . . . . .

But because being here does matter, and because all that's here,
though fleeting, apparently needs us—in some strange way
concerns us. Us, the most fleeting of all. One lifespan
for each thing, single, unique. One time and no more. And for
                                                    us too,
just once. Never again. But this
having once been, even if it's only once:
this having been *earth's* own, seems to be irrevocable.

Thus we drive ourselves onward and struggle toward the goal,
trying to contain it in our bare hands,
in our overscheduled gaze and our speechless heart,
wanting to become it.—To whom do I give it? Best
hold on to everything forever . . . Ah, but to that other realm,
what, alas, can we bring with us? Not our skill at perceiving,
                                                    which was
slowly mastered here, nor any event that here occurred. Not one.

Also die Schmerzen. Also vor allem das Schwersein,
also der Liebe lange Erfahrung, - also
lauter Unsägliches. Aber später,
unter den Sternen, was solls: *die* sind *besser* unsäglich.
Bringt doch der Wanderer auch vom Hange des Bergrands
nicht eine Hand voll Erde ins Tal, die Allen unsägliche,

                                  sondern
ein erworbenes Wort, reines, den gelben und blaun
Enzian. Sind wir vielleicht *hier*, um zu sagen: Haus,
Brücke, Brunnen, Tor, Krug, Obstbaum, Fenster, -
höchstens: Säule, Turm . . . aber zu *sagen*, verstehs,
oh zu sagen so, wie selber die Dinge niemals
innig meinten zu sein. Ist nicht die heimliche List
dieser verschwiegenen Erde, wenn sie die Liebenden drängt,
daß sich in ihrem Gefühl jedes und jedes entzückt?
Schwelle: was ists für zwei
Liebende, daß sie die eigne ältere Schwelle der Tür
ein wenig verbrauchen, auch sie, nach den vielen vorher
und vor den Künftigen . . . , leicht.

Hier ist des *Säglichen* Zeit, *hier* seine Heimat.
Sprich und bekenn. Mehr als je
fallen die Dinge dahin, die erlebbaren, denn,
was sie verdrängend ersetzt, ist ein Tun ohne Bild.
Tun unter Krusten, die willig zerspringen, sobald
innen das Handeln entwächst und sich anders begrenzt.
Zwischen den Hämmern besteht
unser Herz, wie die Zunge
zwischen den Zähnen, die doch,
dennoch, die preisende bleibt.

Wounds, then. Heavy-heartedness, most certainly,
and then the long experience of love,—and finally what
can't be spoken aloud. But later, under the stars,
why do so? *They* are better left *un*spoken.
Nor from high slopes down to the valley does the mountaineer
bring a handful of soil, which he couldn't explain to just anybody,
but instead one pure, hard-earned word—yellow and blue,
the gentian. Might we *be here* just in order to say: House,
Bridge, Wellspring, Gate, Jug, Fruit-tree, Window,—
at the highest level: Column, Tower . . . but, you understand, to
                                        speak them,
oh, to speak them as they *never* within themselves thought
they could prove to be. Isn't it the hidden intention
of this close-mouthed Earth, when it impels lovers onward,
that in their transports, each, yes, each thing should also feel
                                        rapture?
Thresholds: what is it like when two
lovers wear down, just a little, their own older doorsill,
these two in turn, after multitudes coming earlier, and preceding
those still to come . . . so lightly.

This is the era of the sayable, *here* is its homeland.
Speak and make it known. More than ever,
things we might live through are now slipping away, for
what forcibly supplants each of them is a deed without an image,
a deed under a shell, which readily splits, as soon
as the bustle inside outgrows it and redefines its shape.
Our heart puts up with hammer
strokes, just as our tongue
moves between teeth and nevertheless
still continues to sing praises.

Preise dem Engel die Welt, nicht die unsägliche, *ihm*
kannst du nicht großtun mit herrlich Erfühltem; im Weltall,
wo er fühlender fühlt, bist du ein Neuling. Drum zeig
ihm das Einfache, das von Geschlecht zu Geschlechtern
                                        gestaltet,
als ein Unsriges lebt, neben der Hand und im Blick.
Sag ihm die Dinge. Er wird staunender stehn; wie du standest
bei dem Seiler in Rom, oder beim Töpfer am Nil.
Zeig ihm, wie glücklich ein Ding sein kann, wie schuldlos und
                                        unser,
wie selbst das klagende Leid rein zur Gestalt sich entschließt,
dient als ein Ding, oder stirbt in ein Ding -, und jenseits
selig der Geige entgeht. - Und diese, von Hingang
lebenden Dinge verstehn, daß du sie rühmst; vergänglich,
traun sie ein Rettendes uns, den Vergänglichsten, zu.
Wollen, wir sollen sie ganz im unsichtbarn Herzen verwandeln
in - o unendlich - in uns! Wer wir am Ende auch seien.

Erde, ist es nicht dies, was du willst: *unsichtbar*
in uns erstehn? - Ist es dein Traum nicht,
einmal unsichtbar zu sein? - Erde! unsichtbar!
Was, wenn Verwandlung nicht, ist dein drängender Auftrag?
Erde, du liebe, ich will. Oh glaub, es bedürfte
nicht deiner Frühlinge mehr, mich dir zu gewinnen -, *einer*,
ach, ein einziger ist schon dem Blute zu viel.
Namenlos bin ich zu dir entschlossen, von weit her.

To the Angel, praise our world, not the ineffable. *Him*
you won't impress with your noble sentiments. In the overworld,
where he feels with greater feeling, you are a beginner.
                                                    Therefore
bring him simplicity, something shaped from generation to
generation, till it became our own, close at hand, well within
                                                    sight.
Speak to him of *things*. He will be all the more amazed; as you
                                                    were,
by the rope-maker in Rome or the potter beside the Nile.
Show him how joyful a thing can be, how faultless and ours,
how even grief's outcry comes to its conclusion purely in form,
labors as a thing, or dies into a thing—, its soulful revelation
going far beyond a simple violin's. And these things, brought
to life by leaving it, acknowledge that you praise them; ephemeral,
thcy believe in us, the most ephemeral of all, as rescuers.
They would have us wholly transform them into our invisible
                                                    heart,
into—oh for all time!—ourselves. Whoever, at last, we may
                                                    prove to be.

Earth, isn't it this that you desire, to rise up within us
as something *invisible*? Isn't it your dream
one day to be invisible?—Earth, you, invisible!
What task, if not transformation, do you insist that we take up?
Earth, my love, I want that. Oh believe me, no further
springtimes are needed for you to win me over—*one*,
oh, just one is already too much for blood to manage.
Long ago I became your unannounced betrothed.

Immer warst du im Recht, und dein heiliger Einfall
ist der vertrauliche Tod.

Siehe, ich lebe. Woraus? Weder Kindheit noch Zukunft
werden weniger . . . . . Überzähliges Dasein
entspringt mir im Herzen.

You were forever on the side of truth, and your sacred insight
names our trustworthy companion Death.

See, I'm alive. Living for what? Neither childhood nor tomorrow
grows smaller . . . . . Incalculable existence
wells up in this heart.

Die zehnte Elegie

Dass ich dereinst, an dem Ausgang der grimmigen Einsicht,
Jubel und Ruhm aufsinge zustimmenden Engeln.
Daß von den klar geschlagenen Hämmern des Herzens
keiner versage an weichen, zweifelnden oder
reißenden Saiten. Daß mich mein strömendes Antlitz
glänzender mache; daß das unscheinbare Weinen
blühe. O wie werdet ihr dann, Nächte, mir lieb sein,
gehärmte. Daß ich euch knieender nicht, untröstliche
                                        Schwestern,
hinnahm, nicht in euer gelöstes
Haar mich gelöster ergab. Wir, Vergeuder der Schmerzen.
Wie wir sie absehn voraus, in die traurige Dauer,
ob sie nicht enden vielleicht. Sie aber sind ja
unser winterwähriges Laub, unser dunkeles Sinngrün,
eine der Zeiten des heimlichen Jahres -, nicht nur
Zeit -, sind Stelle, Siedelung, Lager, Boden, Wohnort.

Freilich, wehe, wie fremd sind die Gassen der Leid-Stadt,
wo in der falschen, aus Übertönung gemachten
Stille, stark, aus der Gußform des Leeren der Ausguß
prahlt: der vergoldete Lärm, das platzende Denkmal.
O, wie spurlos zerträte ein Engel ihnen den Trostmarkt,
den die Kirche begrenzt, ihre fertig gekaufte:
reinlich und zu und enttäuscht wie ein Postamt am Sonntag.

The Tenth Elegy

That I one day might, in an exodus from dark apprehensions,
sing out in joy and praise to angels voicing approval.
That among the clear-striking hammers of the heart
not one should fail because of weak, tentative or
worn-out strings. That streams running down my face
would make it glow even more. That this reined-in crying
would begin to flower. Nights, oh how dear will you be to me
                                                                then,
despite being brought low. To think I didn't kneel to you more
                                                        eagerly,
disconsolate sisters, and gather you in; didn't, among your
                                                        loosened
tresses, freely lose myself. We who are lavish with our
                                                        afflictions,
how we peer beyond them, in all their mournful lingering,
to see whether they might perhaps conclude. But they are truly
our winter leafage, our dark, evergreen mind,
just *one* of the reticent year's seasons—and more than
a season: they are site, settlement, lair, ground, dwelling.

Alas, how alien to us the alleys of pain's city are,
where, in the unreal calm that follows a thunderbolt,
what is molded solid out of the mold's hollowness
will glitter: in gold-plated uproar, a ravaged monument.
Oh how an Angel would trample clean away the street market
of consolations flanked by the church, all of them for sale
                                                        ready-made:
as tidied and closed and switched off as the Post Office on
                                                        Sunday.

Draußen aber kräuseln sich immer die Ränder von Jahrmarkt.
Schaukeln der Freiheit! Taucher und Gaukler des Eifers!
Und des behübschten Glücks figürliche Schießstatt,
wo es zappelt von Ziel und sich blechern benimmt,
wenn ein Geschickterer trifft. Von Beifall zu Zufall
taumelt er weiter; denn Buden jeglicher Neugier
werben, trommeln und plärrn. Für Erwachsene aber
ist noch besonders zu sehn, wie das Geld sich vermehrt,
anatomisch,
nicht zur Belustigung nur: der Geschlechtsteil des Gelds,
alles, das Ganze, der Vorgang -, das unterrichtet und macht
fruchtbar . . . .
. . . . Oh aber gleich darüber hinaus,
hinter der letzten Planke, beklebt mit Plakaten des ›Todlos‹,
jenes bitteren Biers, das den Trinkenden süß scheint,
wenn sie immer dazu frische Zerstreuungen kaun . . . . ,
gleich im Rücken der Planke, gleich dahinter, ists *wirklich*.
Kinder spielen, und Liebende halten einander, - abseits,
ernst, im ärmlichen Gras, und Hunde haben Natur.
Weiter noch zieht es den Jüngling; vielleicht, daß er eine junge
Klage liebt . . . . . Hinter ihr her kommt er in Wiesen. Sie sagt:
- Weit. Wir wohnen dort draußen . . .
Wo? Und der Jüngling
folgt. Ihn rührt ihre Haltung. Die Schulter, der Hals -,
vielleicht
ist sie von herrlicher Herkunft. Aber er läßt sie, kehrt um,
wendet sich, winkt . . . Was solls? Sie ist eine Klage.

But farther on, the county fair's precincts are bunching up.
Swings lofted in wild abandon! Stunt divers and avid jugglers!
And the shooting-gallery's cartoonish figures standing for
                                              good fortune,
targets that flip and tumble with a tinny ding
when a more practiced marksman scores. Cheered for his
                                              winning strikes,
he staggers on; for booths promoting every sort of novelty
are drumming, are hawking. Something special (for adults only)
is still to be seen, how money breeds more of itself, anatomically,
and for more than mere entertainment: the private parts of
                                              money,
the whole shebang, the how-to—, educational, so that you will be
fruitful and multiply . . . . !
. . . Oh but a little beyond that, just
past the last board fences, where we see posters slapped up for
                                              "Killproof,"
that bitter beer that seems sweet to its drinkers
provided they can at the same time snack on distractions . . . ,
just behind the boards, on the other side of them, is the *real thing*.
Children play, lovers cling to each other—off to one side,
solemn, in meager grass—and dogs answer nature's call.
The young man is impelled farther on; possibly he's in love
with a youthful Lamentation . . . . . He follows her into the
                                              meadows. She says:
"It's far. We live over that way . . . ."
                          Where? And the young man
follows. How she carries herself moves him. Shoulders,
                                      neck—perhaps
she has noble origins. And yet he leaves her, turns, looks
back, waves . . . But then what? Lamentation's who she is.

Nur die jungen Toten, im ersten Zustand
zeitlosen Gleichmuts, dem der Entwöhnung,
folgen ihr liebend. Mädchen
wartet sie ab und befreundet sie. Zeigt ihnen leise,
was sie an sich hat. Perlen des Leids und die feinen
Schleier der Duldung. - Mit Jünglingen geht sie
schweigend.

Aber dort, wo sie wohnen, im Tal, der Älteren eine, der Klagen,
nimmt sich des Jünglings an, wenn er fragt: - Wir waren,
sagt sie, ein Großes Geschlecht, einmal, wir Klagen. Die Väter
trieben den Bergbau dort in dem großen Gebirg; bei Menschen
findest du manchmal ein Stück geschliffenes Ur-Leid
oder, aus altem Vulkan, schlackig versteinerten Zorn.
Ja, der stammte von dort. Einst waren wir reich. -

Und sie leitet ihn leicht durch die weite Landschaft der Klagen,
zeigt ihm die Säulen der Tempel oder die Trümmer
jener Burgen, von wo Klage-Fürsten das Land
einstens weise beherrscht. Zeigt ihm die hohen
Tränenbäume und Felder blühender Wehmut,
(Lebendige kennen sie nur als sanftes Blattwerk);
zeigt ihm die Tiere der Trauer, weidend, - und manchmal
schreckt ein Vogel und zieht, flach ihnen fliegend durchs
                                        Aufschaun,
weithin das schriftliche Bild seines vereinsamten Schreis. -
Abends führt sie ihn hin zu den Gräbern der Alten
aus dem Klage-Geschlecht, den Sibyllen und Warn-Herrn.

Only those who died an early death, in the first phase
of timeless detachment, as they go through the weaning process,
follow her as lovers might. Young women,
she waits for and befriends. Mildly indicates
what she is wearing. Pearls of suffering and sheer veils
of forbearance.—With the young men she proceeds
in silence.

But there, in a valley where they dwell, a matriarch among the
                                             Lamentations
turns to the young man when he questions her. "In the past, we
                                             Lamentations
were," she says, "a great nation. Our forebears dug the mines
                                             up in the high
mountains. Occasionally among humans you find a polished lump
of primal grief, or, in volcanic slag, a piece of rage turned to stone.
Yes, such things came from there. We were once rich."

Gently she guides him through the far landscape of mourning,
showing him temple columns and ruined
fortresses where the Lamentation princes once wisely
ruled the country. She points out lofty trees made of tears
and fields where sorrow has come into flower.
(The living know of it only as tender, early shoots);
she points out sorrow's pastured livestock,—and often
a bird takes fright, streaking straight across their sightlines
to inscribe at a distance the picture of its banished cry.
In the evening she leads him out to the graves where ancestors
of the Lamentation clan are buried, prophetess and prophet alike.

Naht aber Nacht, so wandeln sie leiser, und bald
mondets empor, das über Alles
wachende Grab-Mal. Brüderlich jenem am Nil,
der erhabene Sphinx -: der verschwiegenen Kammer
Antlitz.
Und sie staunen dem krönlichen Haupt, das für immer,
schweigend, der Menschen Gesicht
auf die Waage der Sterne gelegt.

Nicht erfaßt es sein Blick, im Frühtod
schwindelnd. Aber ihr Schaun,
hinter dem Pschent-Rand hervor, scheucht es die Eule. Und sie,
streifend im langsamen Abstrich die Wange entlang,
jene der reifesten Rundung,
zeichnet weich in das neue
Totengehör, über ein doppelt
aufgeschlagenes Blatt, den unbeschreiblichen Umriß.

Und höher, die Sterne. Neue. Die Sterne des Leidlands.
Langsam nennt sie die Klage; - Hier,
siehe: den *Reiter*, den *Stab*, und das vollere Sternbild
nennen sie: *Fruchtkranz*. Dann, weiter, dem Pol zu:
Wiege; Weg; Das Brennende Buch; Puppe; Fenster.
Aber im südlichen Himmel, rein wie im Innern
einer gesegneten Hand, das klar erglänzende >*M*<,
das die Mütter bedeutet . . . . . . -

Doch der Tote muß fort, und schweigend bringt ihn die ältere
Klage bis an die Talschlucht,

As night falls, they move more slowly, and soon
a tomb floats up like the moon
to watch over it all. A sibling to the one close by the Nile,
the Sphinx—: the hushed burial chamber's
visible profile.
And they are awestruck at the kingly head that for all time
has silently weighed our human face
in the balance of the stars.

Disoriented by recent death, his seeing
can't absorb it. But their gaze
startles an owl from behind the pschent's rim. And its wing,
with slow downstrokes, brushes the Sphinx's cheek,
the one fully ripened and rounded.
As it does so, within the new hearing the dead have,
it traces, on a doubled page laid open,
that inexpressible contour.

And on high, the stars. New ones. The stars of pain's country.
Slowly she identifies the Lamentations: "Here,
you see, the *Horseman*, here, the *Standard*, and that denser
constellation,
they call the *Wreath of Fruit*. Then, farther, towards the North
Pole,
the *Cradle*; the *Path*; the *Burning Book*; the *Puppet*; the *Window*.
But there in the southern firmament, pure as the hollow
of a hand that has been blessed, the brilliant sparks of the '*M*'
that signifies Mothers."

Yet the deceased must be on his way, and wordlessly the older
Lamentation leads him to the dale

wo es schimmert im Mondschein:
die Quelle der Freude. In Ehrfurcht
nennt sie sie, sagt: - Bei den Menschen
ist sie ein tragender Strom. -

Stehn am Fuß des Gebirgs.
Und da umarmt sie ihn, weinend.

Einsam steigt er dahin, in die Berge des Ur-Leids.
Und nicht einmal sein Schritt klingt aus dem tonlosen Los.

Aber erweckten sie uns, die unendlich Toten, ein Gleichnis,
siehe, sie zeigten vielleicht auf die Kätzchen der leeren
Hasel, die hängenden, oder
meinten den Regen, der fällt auf dunkles Erdreich im Frühjahr. -

Und wir, die an *steigendes* Glück
denken, empfänden die Rührung,
die uns beinah bestürzt,
wenn ein Glückliches *fällt*.

where it shimmers in moonlight,
the Wellspring of Joy. In fear and trembling,
she names it: "It is," she says, "among humans,
a current that carries great burdens."

They come to a halt at the foot of the peaks,
and there she embraces him in tears.

On his own, he begins to climb the mountains of original pain,
and not once does his step ring out during that untuned mission.

Yet if the eternally dead should alert us to a resemblance,
then consider that they might be gesturing toward the catkins,
those hanging down from leafless hazels, or else
might mention rain that falls on dark soil early in the year.—

And we, who always thought of good fortunes
as *rising*, would experience an emotion
that almost astounds us
when we see a fortunate thing that *falls*.

Notes

Pschent: Rilke's word for the headgear of the Sphinx is not a common word in English and even less common in German. It designates the Egyptian double crown of Upper and Lower Egypt. The actual Egyptian Sphinx is not crowned with one; instead, he wears the folded cloth made familiar by the sarcophagus of Tutankhamun and ancient Egyptian statuary. We know that Rilke spent an entire night outside Cairo near the Sphinx and that he reported seeing an owl during his vigil. If in his poem he chose to ignore what he saw in external reality and to call the Sphinx's headdress a "pschent," a translation should probably retain the word, however odd it is.

LYRICS

You, Neighbor God

You, God, my next-door neighbor, how many times
through long nights I knocked hard to wake you—
did so, because it's not often that I hear you breathe;
then guess: You're by yourself in the living room.
And yet, if you should need something, no one's there—
I mean, to pour a glass of wine for you to taste.
One person is still waiting. Just make a sign.
I'm here, a step away.

By sheer happenstance a paper-thin panel
stands between us. It's possible:
one word from your mouth or even mine—
and that wood breaks through
at once, with no crash or cry.

It's constructed from your portraits.

And your portraits stand before you like names.
And once the light flares up in me, a light
whereby my deepest feelings recognize you,
it squanders its glow on their frames.

And my senses, which instantly dim,
are unhoused and separated from you.

Archaic Torso of Apollo

We hadn't known of a head so strange as his,
Wherein the eyes were ripening like apples.
And yet the torso shines forth like a lamp
In which his gaze, only a little dimmed,

Holds its glow. For otherwise the swell
Of the chest wouldn't blind you, nor a smile
Go towards the light curves of the loins
That testified in flesh to procreation.

Otherwise this stone would stand distorted
Under the shoulders' translucent waterfall;
It wouldn't shimmer like pelts of predators,
Wouldn't break from its confines like a star,
Brightening till no part of you remains
Unseen. The life you led before must change.

Autumn Day

Lord? It is time. Great summer's at an end.
Lay down your shadows on the sundials;
Across the fields unleash a cooler wind.

Tell the last of the fruit to fill and ripen.
Send them two more warm, southerly days,
Push them toward completion then, and chase
Last sweetnesses into the thickened wine.

Those without a house won't build one ever;
Those alone will stay long months alone,
Will wake, will read, write letter after letter;
Will wander up and down the park along
Unsettled paths where falling leaves have blown.

Rilke's Epitaph

Rose, O pure self-contradiction, pleasure—
to be nobody's sleep under so many
eyelids.

LETTERS TO A YOUNG POET

The Sixth Letter

Rome, 23 December, 1903

My dear Mr. Kappus,

You shouldn't remain without a greeting from me
as Christmas arrives, a time when, surrounded by
celebrations, you must be feeling your solitude more
intensely. Yet when you realize that it is in fact a great
thing, that's something to be glad about. For what, you
might ask, would solitude be if it didn't have aspects of
greatness? There is only one solitude, great, and not easy
to bear. And almost all of us go through periods when we
would happily exchange it for any sort of socializing, no
matter how shallow or cheap, indeed, for the least hint
of common interest from any second-rate or thoroughly
unworthy person. . . . Yet perhaps these are precisely the
times when solitude grows up; for its maturing is painful
as the growing-up a boy experiences, and as sorrowful
as the early days of spring. But that shouldn't mislead
you. What's needed is just one thing: solitude—great,
inward solitude. Going into oneself and not meeting
anyone for hours—that's what you must manage to do.
Being alone just as you were as a child, when adults were
pacing around, concerned with what appeared to be grand
and important merely because they looked so busy and
because you didn't understand any of their actions.

And when in time we understand that their pursuits
are insignificant, that their professions are ossified and
no longer connected to life, why not then still regard all

of it as a child would, as if we were looking at something foreign, far outside the depths of our own world and the breadth of our solitude, which *itself* is your work, your rank, your vocation. Why would anyone care to replace the child's wise abstention from understanding with their bickering and contempt, given that *not* understanding such things is finally being on one's own, while bickering and contempt are implicated in all that one wants to leave behind. Consider, sir, the world you carry inside yourself, and name these thoughts whatever you like: let them be a remembrance of your childhood or else a longing for a future of your own; be observant of what rises up inside and put that above all the things you notice around you. Your most inward events deserve all your love; you must somehow work towards them and not waste too much time, or too much falter in courage as you clarify your stance towards humankind. Who told you that you especially have one at all?—I know, your profession is hard and full of things antagonistic to you; I foresaw your heartache and knew it would at some point emerge. Now that it has, there is nothing I can say to comfort you, I can only suggest that you ask yourself whether *all* professions are not like that, weighed down with demands, with enmity towards the individual, steeped, so to speak, in a contempt for those who find themselves gloomy and wordless before some arid set of duties. The situation in which you have to live now isn't charged with more formalities, prejudices and false notions than any other situation; and, if some of those seem to promise greater freedom, none is, in itself, wide and spacious and in touch with things that the fully authentic life consists of. Only the solitary person is subjected, like a material object, to the most fundamental laws. And when he goes out at sunrise, or gazes at an evening crowded with event, when he experiences what is happening there, all preoccupations fall away from him as if he had died, no matter that he stands in the midst of life at its purest. What you are forced to undergo as an officer, dear Mr. Kappus, you would have felt just as much in any other standard profession. Yes, even if, outside any position of employment, you had attempted to find a facile and independent contact with society, you wouldn't have been spared this persistent sensation.—It is everywhere the same, but that is no reason to be anxious or sad. If you can't find common ground with other people, try to be close to *things*. They will not abandon you. And nights are still there, along with winds that move through the trees, across many lands. You will find within the world of material objects and among animals that they are always filled with occurrences that you can participate in. And children are still the same as they were when you were a child, sad and happy in much the same way. And if you think of your childhood, once again you will live in their midst, among the solitary children, while the adults are practically nothing, their worthiness not worth much.

And if thinking of childhood brings you fear and anguish as you recall its bygone quiet and simplicity, along with the consideration that you can no longer believe in God (who is everywhere manifest in childhood), then ask yourself, dear Mr. Kappus, if you have indeed lost God. Isn't it much more the case that you have never yet possessed him? For when would that have been so? Do you believe that a child could grasp him—him whom adults bear only with a great struggle, just as his heft crushes the old? Do you believe that a person who truly has him could lose him like a little pebble? Don't you suppose instead that anyone who once had him could only be lost by *him*? But if you acknowledge that, during your childhood, he did not exist, and not before that, either, if you suspect that Christ was misled by his longing, and Mohammed deceived by his presumption—and if you, in fear and trembling, feel that in the present also he does not exist, even at this moment when we are talking about him—how, then, are you justified in missing this person (who never existed) like someone deceased, and how can you search for him as though he had been lost?

Why don't you think of him as the One Who Is to Come, the one who has forever been approaching, a future entity that will someday arrive as the full fruition of a tree whose leaves we are. What stops you from casting his birth forward into the coming ages and living your life as a painful but beautiful moment in the chronicle of a great pregnancy? Don't you see how all that happens is always and ever a beginning? And could it not be His beginning, given that to originate is in itself beautiful? If he is the final perfection, wouldn't what is lesser necessarily exist before he does, so that he can choose from fullness and surplus? Shouldn't he be the Ultimate, so that he can contain everything else in himself? And what purpose or meaning would we have if the one we are longing for had already been here?

As bees collect honey, so do we gather what is sweetest from all things and use it to construct him. We will start even with lesser, with nondescript things, so long as what we do arises out of love. We start with labor and the rest that follows it; we start by keeping silent, or with a small, solitary joy; we start with everything we do alone, with no one joining in or helping us. We are the starting point of one whom we will not live to see, no more than our forebears could live long enough to see us. And yet those people long since gone still exist in us, as investment, as a duty placed on our destiny; as rushing blood, and as a gesture that reaches up out of the depths of time. Is there anything that can take away your hope that you will one day exist in him, who is the farthest forward, the outermost? Celebrate Christmas, dear Mr. Kappus, with the worshipful feeling that perhaps your mortal anguish is precisely what he needs in order to begin. These days of transition themselves are perhaps the time when everything in you is struggling towards him, just as you once as a child breathlessly struggled towards him. Be patient and with no ill will, acknowledge that the least we can do is to make it no more difficult for him to exist than the earth manages to do for spring when it is ready to come.

And be cheerful and confident.

Yours,

Rainer Maria Rilke

The Eighth Letter

Borgeby gård, Flädie, Sweden

12 August 1904

I want to speak to you again for a moment, dear Mr.
Kappus, though there is practically nothing I can say that
might help; in fact, I can hardly find anything at all useful.
You have undergone many sorrowful events, heavy ones, and
they have now passed. And you say that even this process
was difficult and jarring for you. But please ask yourself
whether these great sorrows haven't instead passed *through*
you. Whether perhaps many things within you haven't
been transformed; whether, in some part, deep within your
being, you haven't undergone serious changes during your
period of sadness. The only sorrows that are dangerous and
morbid are those we bring with us into the social sphere,
trying to drown them out. As with illnesses that are treated
carelessly and irrationally, they simply retreat and after a
brief interim break out again even more dreadfully than
before. They assemble within us and are some sort of life,
life that is unlived, scorned, lost—life that can put you to
death. If only we could see farther than the limits of our
understanding, even a little over and beyond the barriers set
in front of all we suspect, then we might possibly bear our
sorrows with a trust greater than what we bring to our joys.
For these are the instants when something new has entered
us, something unknown. Our feelings are struck dumb with
shy self-consciousness, everything inside us takes a step
back, a silence steals in, and the new thing, never before
known, stands at the center of it all and remains silent.

I would say all our sorrows are moments of stress, which we experience as a sort of paralysis because we can no longer hear the life of our alienated feelings. Because we are alone with the strange thing that has entered us; because all that we trust and are accustomed to is for an instant taken from us; because we stand in the midst of a transition, where we can't continue to stand. Because the sadness also goes onward: the new thing inside us, this newly added thing, has entered our heart, has gone into its innermost chamber and then isn't there anymore—is already in our blood. And we haven't arrived at what it really was. One could easily be made to believe that nothing has happened, and yet we have been transformed, as a house where a guest has entered is transformed. We can't say who has come, and we may never know; but many signs suggest that the future has entered us in a manner that allows it to be transformed in us, long before its actual arrival. And that is why it is so important to be solitary and observant when we are sad: because the apparently uneventful and motionless instant when our future strides into us is so much closer to life than that other loud and random moment when what happens to us seems to come from outside. The quieter we are, the more patient and open we are to our sorrow, the more deeply and unerringly this new thing can enter us; and the more we acquire it for ourselves, the more it becomes *our* destiny. And we will join with it on a later day when it "happens" (that is, goes out of us to other people), transformed into our deepest inwardness and close to the heart. And that is needed. It is needed—and it will move farther and farther towards our development—so that nothing strange will overcome us, but only what has for a long time belonged to us.

People have already had to reconsider so many concepts concerning the laws of motion; and they will eventually realize that what we call fate does not come into them from outside but instead emerges *from* them. It is only because so many people have not absorbed and transformed their fate while they were inhabiting it that they haven't realized what was emerging from them; it was so alien to them that, in their extreme fright, they thought it must have entered them just at that moment, because they swore that they had never before found anything like that inside themselves. As we've long been mistaken about the motion of the sun, we are still deceiving ourselves about the movement of what is to come. The future holds fast, dear Mr. Kappus, but we are moving in infinite space.

How could it not be hard for us?

And when we talk about solitude again, it becomes clearer that this is finally not something that you can choose or leave aside. We are alone. You can fool yourself and pretend it's not so. That's all. But how much better is it to acknowledge that we are alone—indeed, to take it as a point of departure. That will of course give us vertigo; for all the reference points our eyes depended on are taken away from us, there is nothing nearby, and all distant things are infinitely distant. Anyone who was thrust out of his room, with little preparation or transition, and taken up to the height of a large mountain would have to feel something similar: an insecurity without equal; a surrender to the Unnamable would almost destroy him. He would expect to fall or fling himself out into space or be shattered into a thousand pieces: what an immense lie his brain would have to invent in order to catch up with and clarify the state of his senses. Thus, for those who become lonely, all distances, all dimensions change; Many of these changes take place suddenly, and, as with that man on the top of the mountain, unusual illusions and strange sensations emerge, which seem to exceed everything bearable. But it is necessary for us to experience that, too. We must accept our existence no matter how far it travels. Everything, even the unheard of, must be possible in it. That's fundamentally the only courageous act required of us: being fearless before the strangest, most fanciful, and most inexplicable things we may encounter. The fact that people were cowardly in this manner has done infinite harm to life; the encounters called "apparitions," the entire "spirit world" (so called), and death, all these things closely related to us, have been driven so far out of life by our perpetual warding them off, that the senses with which we might have managed to grasp those things have become stunted. Not to mention God. But the fear of the inexplicable has not only made the individual's existence poorer, but the relationships between people have also been constricted—as though these were lifted out of the riverbed of infinite possibilities and placed on a barren shore where nothing happens. For it is not lethargy alone that makes human relationships repeat themselves, time after time, into unspeakable monotony and stultification; it is the fear of any new, unforeseeable experience that one doesn't feel strong enough for. Only those who are prepared for everything, who exclude nothing, even what is most enigmatic, will experience a relationship with another person as something fully alive and create something out of their own being. For when we consider this being of the individual as a larger or smaller room, it turns out that most people only get to know one corner of their room, a window seat or a track where they pace up and down. That way, they have a certain security. And yet it is so much more human, that dangerous insecurity that compels the prisoners in Poe's stories to feel their way around the confines of their dreadful dungeons and not diminish the inexpressible horror of their imprisonment. But we are not prisoners. There are no traps and snares waiting for us, and there is nothing that might frighten or afflict us. We are placed in life as the element we are most in keeping with. Moreover, through millennia of adaptation, we have become so similar to this life that, if we keep quiet, we are, through a happy mimicry of everything around us, hardly to be distinguished from it.

We have no reason to distrust our world, because it is not against us. If it holds terrors, the terror is ours; if it has abysses, then these abysses belong to us; if there are dangers, then we must try to love them. And if we will only construct our life according to the principle telling us that we must always hold fast to what is difficult, then the things that now appear to us as the strangest become the most familiar and the most trustworthy. How should we forget those ancient myths found at the beginning of all nations, stories of dragons who at the last moment turn into princesses. Maybe all the dragons in our lives are princesses just waiting to see us act with beauty and courage. Perhaps everything that frightens us is in the deepest sense a helpless thing that wants us to help it.

So you must not be afraid, dear Mr. Kappus, when a sorrow in front of you, bigger than any you have yet seen, rises up; or when disquiet, like light and cloud shadows, passes over your hands and over all your actions. You must think that something is happening to you, that

life has not forgotten you, that it holds you in its hands;
it will not drop you. Why do you want to exclude all
restlessness, pain, and sadness from your life, since you
don't know what effects these states of mind are having on
you? Why do you care to pursue the question of where it
all comes from and where it is going? That is, since you
know that you are in a transitional stage and wish more
than anything else to be transformed. If something in
your response to this borders on pathology, remember
that disease is the means by which an organism frees
itself from what is foreign. All you have to do is help it
to be ill, to have the entire illness and to break out with
it; because that is how it recovers. So much, dear Mr.
Kappus, is happening in you now. You must be as patient as
someone who is ill and just as confident as someone who is
convalescing—because you are perhaps both. Furthermore,
you are also the doctor who has to monitor himself.
But there are many days in every illness, so the doctor
can do nothing but wait. And that's what you, insofar
as you are your own doctor, have to do before all else.

Don't pay too much attention to yourself. Don't draw
hasty conclusions from what happens to you; just let it
happen. Otherwise, it is too easy for you to look with
disapproval (from the moral standpoint) at your past,
which, of course, is involved in everything you now
experience. The ordeals, wishes, and longings of your
boyhood are at work in you, but they are not what you
remember and condemn. The extraordinary circumstances
of a lonely and helpless childhood are so difficult, so
complicated, so exposed to so many influences, and at the
same time so removed from all actual life contexts, that,
where a vice enters into them, one should not simply call

it a vice. You have to be very careful with names; so often it is the mere name of a crime that a life crashes into, and not the nameless personal action itself—which may have been a very definite necessity of that life and could easily be absorbed by it. And the energy being expended seems so excessive only because you overvalue the victory; it is not the "great thing" you have achieved, though you are right about how you feel. The great thing is that you already had something that you were able to substitute for that sham, something true and real. Without it, even your victory would have been only a moral reflex without much significance; but, no, it has become a part of your life. Your life, dear Mr. Kappus, which I think of and have hopes for.

Do you remember how that life from childhood on has longed for "great deeds"? I see how it now longs for great deeds, yes, but beyond them to even greater ones. That's the reason it remains arduous, but also why it will not stop growing.

And if there is one more thing I ought to say, it is this: Do not imagine that the person trying to comfort you just now lives effortlessly behind those simple and calm words that sometimes seem to do you good. His life has much hardship and sadness and lags far behind you. But if that were not the case, he would never have been able to find those words.

Your Rainer Maria Rilke

ACKNOWLEDGMENTS

First, I wish to thank Clare Hall of the University of Cambridge for a residence fellowship allowing me to make use of the University Library's research facilities and for the collegiality I experienced while in residence. I am grateful for the kind assistance of Professor David Midgley of the German Faculty, St. John's College, who led me to many helpful secondary sources and offered encouragement along the way. He read and commented on several of the Elegies as I translated them, as did Professor Thomas Austenfeld of the American Literature Faculty of the University of Fribourg. Other readers offered useful comments on the work as it progressed. I thank Marilyn Hacker and especially Paul Eprile, who provided carefully annotated responses to the entire work. These readers are, however, not responsible for any errors or infelicities that the final version might contain. It was a pleasure to see parts of the work appear in literary journals, and thanks are due the editors who published them in *The Alabama Literary Review*, *The Arkansas International*, *Arts & Letters*, *The Asheville Poetry Review*,

The Hudson Review, Literary Matters, The New Criterion, and *Spoke*. Finally, I am grateful for the assistance of my agent Steven Salpeter of Curtis Brown, Ltd., and to Jill Bialosky at W. W. Norton for her deft editorial work on the project and for her enthusiasm, which was a welcome boost during the process of its completion.

SELECTED BIBLIOGRAPHY

Ulrich Baer, *The Rilke Alphabet*. Translated by Andrew Hamilton. Fordham University Press, 2014.

Frank Baron, Ernst S. Dick, and Warren Maurer, editors, *Rilke: The Alchemy of Alienation*. University Press of Kansas, 1980.

William Gass, *Reading Rilke: Reflections on the Problems of Translation*. Alfred A. Knopf, 2000.

Wolfgang Leppmann, *Rilke: A Life*. Translated from the German by Russell M. Stockman, verse translations by Richard Exner. Fromm International Publishing Corporation, 1984.

Roger Paulin and Peter Hutchinson, editors, *Rilke's "Duino Elegies."* Duckworth & Ariadne Press, 1996.

Rainer Maria Rilke: Briefe, herausgegeben vom Rilke-Archiv in Weimar, in Verbindung mit Ruth Sieber-Rilke besorgt durch Karl Altheim. Insel Verlag, 1950.

Rainer Maria Rilke, *The Dark Interval: Letters on Loss, Grief, and Transformation*. Translated by Ulrich Baer. Random House, 2018.

Rainer Maria Rilke, *Rainer Maria Rilke: Werke: Kommentierte Ausgabe*, 4 volumes. Edited by Manfred Engel, Ulrich Fülleborn, Horst Nalewski, and August Stahl. Insel Verlag, 1996.

Rainer Maria Rilke, *Sämtliche Werke*, 7 vols. Edited by Ernst Zinn and Ruth Sieber-Rilke. Insel Verlag, 1955–1997.

Rainer Maria Rilke, *Selected Poems, with Parallel German Text*. Translated by Susan Ranson and Marielle Sutherland. Edited and with an introduction and notes by Robert Vilain. Oxford University Press, 2011.

Rainer Maria Rilke and Lou Andreas-Salomé, *Briefwechsel*. Insel Verlag, 1952.

Frank Wood, *Rainer Maria Rilke: The Ring of Forms*. University of Minnesota Press, 1958.

ABOUT THE TRANSLATOR

Alfred Corn has published eleven books of poems, the most recent titled *Unions* (2014) and two novels, the second titled *Miranda's Book* (2014). His three collections of essays are *The Metamorphoses of Metaphor*, *Atlas: Selected Essays: 1989–2007*, and *Arks & Covenants*. He has received the Guggenheim, the NEA, an Award in Literature from the Academy of Arts and Letters, and one from the Academy of American Poets. He has taught at Yale, Columbia, the University of Cincinnati, and UCLA. In 2013 he was made a Life Fellow of Clare Hall, Cambridge. In 2016 Spain's Chamán Ediciones published *Rocinante*, a selection of his work translated in Spanish, the same translation appearing the following year in Mexico under the title *Antonio en el desierto*. He has published translations from classical Greek, Latin, French, German, Italian, Russian, Chinese, and Spanish. In October of 2016, *Roads Taken*, a celebration of the 40th anniversary of Alfred Corn's first book, *All Roads at Once*, was held at Poets' House in New York City, and in November 2017 he was inducted into the Georgia Writers' Hall of Fame. He lives in Providence, Rhode Island.